IMAGES
of America

New Jersey's
Masonic Lodges

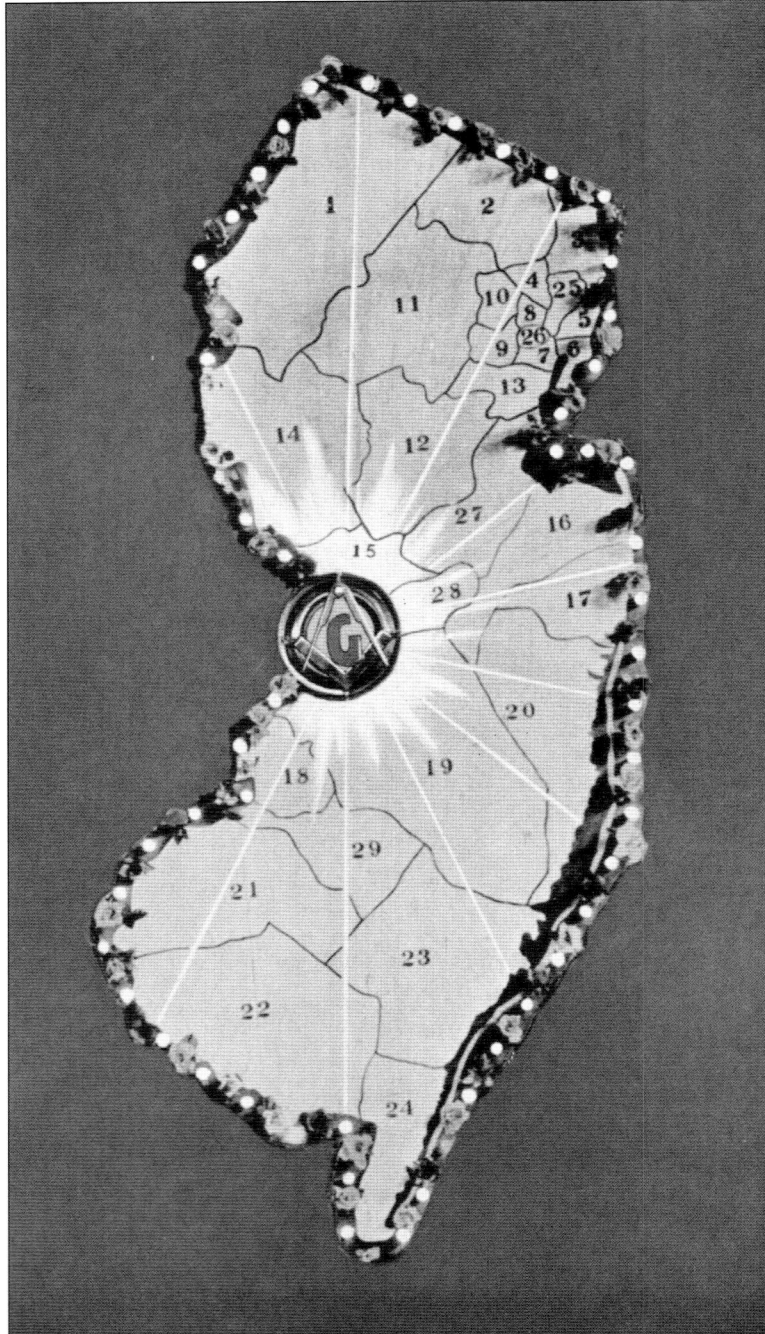

This map from 1935 shows the Masonic districts of New Jersey. That year, the fraternity managed 29 districts with a membership of 85,870 through 278 Lodges. Today, the Grand Lodge of State of New Jersey oversees 116 individual Lodges with 17,278 members through 19 districts. (Courtesy of Grand Lodge of New Jersey, 1936.)

ON THE COVER: This photograph, presumably of the trustees and officers of the Morristown Masonic Temple Association (MMTA), was likely taken on August 25, 1931, at the formal opening of the building. The MMTA was composed of several Masonic organizations that raised funds, maintained the building, and shared ownership of the property. Today, only Cincinnati Lodge No. 3 remains. (Courtesy of Cincinnati Lodge No. 3.)

IMAGES
of America

NEW JERSEY'S
MASONIC LODGES

Erich Morgan Huhn
Foreword by MW Glenn Trautmann, PGM

ARCADIA
PUBLISHING

Published by Arcadia Publishing
Charleston, South Carolina

Printed in the United States of America

Library of Congress Control Number: 2019940192

For all general information, please contact Arcadia Publishing:
Telephone 843-853-2070
Fax 843-853-0044
E-mail sales@arcadiapublishing.com
For customer service and orders:
Toll-Free 1-888-313-2665

Visit us on the Internet at www.arcadiapublishing.com

*To RW Thomas Watson Thornton, PGO (1928–2019),
a scholar, Mason, and friend, whose encouragement
and mentoring inspired this work.*

CONTENTS

FOREWORD

In this great brotherhood, when we speak about a Masonic lodge, we are not necessarily talking about a building but rather the brethren who compose the lodge. As members of a lodge, the group oftentimes forms their own personality. So, too, do the structure and designs of a Masonic edifice shape the community's opinions of our fraternity.

In this book, Erich attempts to delve into Masonic structures that our lodges call home. With many of our lodges merging to run a more efficient fraternity, we are grateful that the history of so many of our remarkable buildings will be preserved for future generations.

Many of New Jersey's Masonic lodges have served multiple uses over the duration of their existence. Some have served as municipal buildings while others have opened their doors to civic groups, such as the boy scouts and the girl scouts. And as most know, we have always allowed other Masonic organizations to make use of our edifices.

I hope you enjoy this book, and I personally thank Erich for his hard work in saving an important part of the history of our brotherhood.

Sincerely and fraternally,
Glenn R. Trautmann, Past Grand Master

ACKNOWLEDGMENTS

The poet and Anglican cleric John Donne wrote in 1624, "No man is an island entire of itself." To say any published or scholarly work is the sole creation of one mind would be to negate the impact and influence of others. Thus is true for this work.

First and foremost, I would like to thank Thomas "Tom" Watson Thornton, who is responsible for introducing me to Freemasonry back in 2012 while I was interning at the Morris County Historical Society. Tom was a founding member of NJ LORE (Lodge of Masonic Research & Education) No. 1786 and a leader in Masonic research. Tom's dedication and research on Freemasonry helped inspire my passion for the subject, and this book is in no small part a result of his influence.

In terms of institutions and organizations, I would like to thank the New York Historical Society, the Library of Congress, the Newark Public Library, and the Meadowlands Museum for all supplying images for this work. In particular, I would like to thank the staff at the North Jersey History & Genealogy Center in Morristown for their help on this project and all the other work I have bothered them with over the years. Most importantly, I would like to thank the Grand Lodge of New Jersey and Cincinnati Lodge No. 3 for supplying the lion share of the images. Additionally, I would like to thank NJ LORE No. 1786, whose members I have just recently met and proved immediate friends that I look forward to working with on future endeavors.

Individually; I would like to thank RW Glenn Trautmann for the wonderful foreword; Drew Jardine and all building trustees throughout the state who work tirelessly maintaining and preserving the beautiful lodge buildings; My friends Chris Cregan, Amy Curry, Joen Ferrari, Pat Goodfriend, Dan Gross, Maxine and Jonathan Lurie, Anna and Rory Macleod, Shane Paules, Mike Tighe, and everyone who had to endure my endless musings on this subject; my friends at St. Peter's Episcopal Church; my coworkers, especially Melanie Bump, Jack Carroll, Samantha Hartford, Katie Humphreys, Maureen Harrison, and Maressa McFarlane; and most of all, my brother (biologically and fraternally) Tyler, parents Karen and Arthur, and grandparents Joan and Roger Morgan, who all have kindly and patiently entertained my scholarly pursuits.

For those I have forgotten, my humble apologies.

INTRODUCTION

Drive through most any town throughout the country, and you may find a simple (often blue) square and compass sign by the town line. These signs are not alone; the Elks, Moose, and Eagles present a menagerie of organizations drawn from the animal kingdom, while the Woodsmen, Foresters, and Grange grew from occupational themes. But the Freemasons, with their simple square and compass, remain one of the largest and strongest fraternal organizations not just in the country but also throughout the world. In 2017, the Masonic Service Association of North America reported that there were over one million members, with estimates of around six million internationally. This organization, parodied in cartoons like *The Simpsons* with "the Stonecutters" and dramatized in works like Dan Brown's *Angels & Demons*, is often thought of by the public as a "secret society." The very words invoke thoughts of secret rituals in dark rooms or plots for world domination. The reality is quite different—would a secret international organization really have signs advertising meeting times?

The Freemasons represent one of the oldest and most successful fraternal organizations in human history. Founded in the Age of the Enlightenment, Freemasonry expanded throughout the world on the ideals of brotherly love, relief, and truth. The purpose of this work is twofold, first to provide a concise history of the Freemasons in New Jersey (largely below through the introduction and chapter introductions) and second to draw light to some of the beautiful structures and (physical) landmarks of Freemasonry throughout the Garden State. Other works have taken a more scholarly approach to both these subjects, for which the bibliography appended should, hopefully, serve as a worthy guide. This book is just one humble attempt at placing down in ink and paper the long and impressive history of New Jersey's Masonic Lodges.

The history of Freemasonry has been a topic that has both confounded and intrigued members and a handful of scholars ever since the organization's founding. Most difficult, perhaps, is divorcing the *history* and the *mythos*. For many works on the history of Freemasonry, particularly those produced from within the fraternity, the realities often are obscured by the vivid ritualistic origins that are promoted through the fraternity's rituals. Professional scholars have only just scratched the surface of the history of Freemasonry, and much work remains to be done, both in understanding the role of Freemasonry in history and in disseminating the reality to members and the public alike. Yet, even with that said, the real history of Freemasonry that has survived through the archives presents a fascinating tale of its own.

As early as the mid-17th century, records exist that corroborate the establishment of Masonic Lodges that were free of the "operative" labor of physical stonemasons. These "speculative" lodges were found throughout Great Britain and claimed membership largely from genteel and privileged backgrounds. Through these early lodges, members were initiated through rituals that provided an allegorical link to stonemasons and traced the organization back to the time of King Solomon.

By the 18th century, these speculative lodges, which had no connection to any building trades, began organizing themselves through what became known as a "Grand Lodge." In an attempt to create order from chaos and establish a centralized governing authority the first Grand Lodge was established in London sometime between 1717 and 1721 (recent scholarship has called into question the long-established date of 1717). With the Age of Enlightenment stirring the passions of the upper-middle classes, Freemasonry emerged as a popular outlet for the new enlightened *philosophés* of Europe. By the Age of Revolution, what is referred to as "the Craft" had spread and developed throughout Europe and North America.

In the United States, Freemasonry had early roots in New Jersey. The first known Freemason in the New World was John Skene, a Scotsman who immigrated to New Jersey in the late 17th century. As early as the 1730s, Masonic activity was noted across the Delaware in Philadelphia and the first Provincial Grand Master in North America had been created in the person of Daniel Coxe Jr. (although very little is known about Coxe, and it is believed that he never acted on his authority as a Provincial Grand Master). By the time of the American Revolution, Freemasonry had become a visible component in American Colonial life, with membership including many colonial elites seeking the refinements of European society in the rugged colonial frontier.

With the Revolution came many changes to Freemasonry. Besides an internal schism between "Modern" and "Ancient" Freemasons, the craft was faced with a peculiar problem when ties with Great Britain were cut. During the Revolution, this quagmire was addressed by members serving in the Continental Army while wintering at Morristown in 1779. At a celebration of St. John the Evangelist, members from the various Provincial Grand Lodges which had been established by the Grand Lodge in London met. The ensuing "Morristown Convention" saw the proposal of a "Supreme" Grand Lodge over the rebelling colonies that would be independent of British influence. Although the idea of a single Grand Lodge ultimately failed to gain traction, the seeds of Grand Lodge sovereignty had been planted.

Over the next seven years, Freemasonry enjoyed surprising stability. As New Jersey was thrown into the throngs of war, claiming host to more battles and skirmishes than any other state, several Masonic lodges were established. By the time peace came, Masonic Provincial Grand Lodges had largely turned to self-rule. Within a decade of the Treaty of Paris, 12 of the original 13 colonies had established independent Grand Lodges (Delaware would finally establish a Grand Lodge in 1806). The Freemasons of New Jersey gathered for the New Brunswick Conventions held over the winter of 1785–1786 and established what would become the Grand Lodge of the Most Ancient and Honorable Society of Free and Accepted Masons for the State of New Jersey.

Yet Freemasonry did not always enjoy unbridled growth. In the 1820s, after the mysterious disappearance and murder of William Morgan, public opinion turned against the fraternity. Morgan had published *Illustrations of Masonry*, an exposé, in 1826 and went missing soon after. Though this was hardly the first exposé or public accounting of the purported "secrets" of Freemasonry, the events made news across the new nation and led to the establishment of the Anti-Masonic Party, the country's first third party. What became known as the Morgan Affair lasted from the mid-1820s to the end of the 1830s and saw widespread decline in membership and participation. Many lodges throughout the country closed their doors, some to reestablish themselves by the 1840s and 1850s. By the time of the Civil War, Freemasonry had stabilized and was once again growing in popularity.

The Golden Age of Fraternalism would come after the Civil War. As veterans looked to replicate the comradeship they had experienced in wartime, and exploited workers sought social and financial safety, fraternal organizations saw a huge boom. Countless new fraternal groups emerged as friendly and benevolent societies that offered aid or insurance benefits. For Freemasonry, the formalized structures of benefit societies were never instituted although throughout the country Grand lodges began establishing "Masonic Homes" for aged or destitute members and the tenets of "brotherly love" and "relief" often reared themselves in the form of charity to members. This period would continue through World War I and only ended with the Great Depression as the nation was reeled by economic downturn and energies geared toward the coming war.

By the end of World War II, Freemasonry had regained traction among the Greatest Generation. Just as members flocked to the many fraternal organizations after the Civil War, the period after

World War II saw what has become the Golden Age of Freemasonry. This period saw the largest growth in numbers, with the organization peaking membership just over four million members nationwide in 1959. This great influx of members meant a huge expansion, as Masonic Lodges (and their buildings) sprang up across the country.

Over the last six decades, however, Freemasonry has slowly declined in members. Today, the Grand Lodge of New Jersey maintains a membership of just over 17,000 across 116 lodges. While this number has stabilized over the last decade, it is a far cry from the golden age. With the general decline in participation throughout society, Freemasonry has faced the same problems of aging membership and membership retention as other voluntary associations in recent years. Yet there is still hope. Campaigns like "2B1Ask1" have demystified membership, and popular cultural references have inspired a new generation of members looking for something in an age of impersonal (mostly virtual) contact. Amid the troughs and peaks of popularity, Freemasonry has endured, in part because of the fraternity's continual presence within the community.

Intimately linked to the presence of Masonic charity in a community is the physical presence of the many buildings that the Freemasons have erected throughout the country. These landmarks can be found from New York to Los Angeles and in the countless towns, cities, and communities in between. From the earliest days of the Grand Lodge era, the building of physical lodge structures has played an important role in linking the fraternity to the community, and today, as communities are absorbed into larger and larger collectives, the local lodge serves as a bastion of old-school fraternal communities.

At the same time, the very ritual of Freemasonry itself required members to envision the physical Lodge meeting room as a representation of King Solomon's Temple. Drawing on this ancient past, Masonic initiation ritual focuses on the building of this greatest edifice. For members, the lodge room represents the Sanctum Sanctorum, and the Worshipful Master of the Lodge plays the allegorical representation of King Solomon himself. Although early Freemasons may have had to use considerable imagination to conger this staging, later Lodges would go to great expense constructing and decorating lodge buildings.

As evident in the ensuing chapters, the buildings that Masonic lodges have occupied span a vast array. From simple frame buildings or rented rooms above taverns and inns to expansive multiuse facilities, the buildings have played important roles as community centers. In the early days of Freemasonry, Lodges met largely in rented spaces, though after the establishment of the Grand Lodge in 1786, and with the increased membership during the Early Republic, some Lodges established small and humble buildings throughout the state. This trend continued in New Jersey through the early part of the 19th century, but by the Gilded Age, New Jersey Freemasons sought to solidify their roots, and the great building spree began. Throughout the country, fraternal organizations built headquarters and established a variety of lodges, aeries, councils, and temples. This building craze continued largely through to the Great Depression and coincided with the Golden Age of Fraternalism. With the Golden Age of Freemasonry in the 1950s, the building boom took off once again. The variety and scale of the buildings left by the Freemasons present an interesting look into the way Freemasons viewed themselves and the role their organization played within American social life.

Throughout the early period of Masonic history, the vast majority of Lodges met in rented space above taverns, private homes, or in spaces within churches. During the colonial period, this was as much a matter of economics as it was pragmatic; Lodges lacked the funding, resources, or even the interest to build separate structures to house the growing fraternity. Although Freemasonry was largely unorganized in colonial New Jersey, this was seen in both New York City and Philadelphia where the established Provincial Grand Lodges in those leading cities met in humbler apartments. Even across the pond in London, Grand Lodge meetings were held at taverns in rented rooms upstairs. In a period before mass-produced consumer goods, the need for space to display Masonic symbols or paraphernalia simply did not exist. This trend continued through the Early Republic period, and by the time of the Morgan Affair, the fraternity as a whole was largely spared the expense that would have entailed maintaining physical structures as many of the Lodges "went dark" or folded altogether.

Yet as American prosperity increased after the Civil War, the need for distinct space became apparent. At the same time, commercial firms emerged that began selling a wide array of Masonic paraphernalia and supplies. Anything from large decorative columns referenced in the ritual to elaborate furniture sets designed for the lodge officers and members all could be purchased through mail-order. This saw an end to the days of crowded lodge rooms where symbols were sometimes drawn directly on wooden floors in chalk or simple paper and wood cutouts sufficed for decorations. With the emergence of American consumerism, Freemasonry embraced the new elaborate trappings that became available. The concurrent increase in membership meant the organization could support the purchase and maintenance of their own buildings. The most typical form of these early lodge buildings took shape as multistory (generally three or four) structures in the center of town. While the first floor could be used to generate rental income from shops, the upper floors could be reserved to house fraternal spaces that included collation rooms, lounges, and the all-important lodge room. These buildings also became popular town centers, often housing post offices or general stores and, with other fraternal organizations, sharing the ceremonial lodge rooms. At the same time, many Lodges were hesitant to take on the burden of managing a property and continued to rent spaces, though by the late 19th century, the idea of a Masonic Lodge meeting in a tavern or inn was by no means standard, and even Lodges without buildings of their own had moved into rented spaces in commercial buildings.

By the turn of the 20th century, however, the boom in membership meant many Lodges outgrew rented or shared spaces. Over the next three decades, Masonic Lodges throughout the nation would go on to build elaborate buildings that met the unique demands of the growing fraternity. Large single-purpose buildings were erected in a variety of architectural styles. These new buildings were typically called "temples" in reference to the Temple of King Solomon, which the structures were to symbolically reflect. Inside, members enjoyed amble space in parlors and libraries along with dedicated spaces to change into Masonic regalia. Often these buildings were constructed in conjunction with multiple lodges or other Masonic-related "Appendant Bodies," like the York Rite. These spaces became important centers of Masonic social activity and would be abuzz with meetings and events throughout the week. Typically, this second form of Masonic lodge was designed around a lodge room on the second floor with a collation room below. Large organs and elaborate decorations could be displayed to add the distinct flair of a Masonic atmosphere. These buildings are among the most recognizable Masonic edifices in the state. With large columns and stately architecture, the buildings were often located around the town centers and business districts and were often built with expensive (or at least very good imitation) materials that added to their grace and grandeur.

As Freemasonry entered into its own golden age after the World War II, however, the large and expensive Masonic lodge buildings which had dominated the first half of the 20th century gave way to smaller more economical structures. These postwar lodge buildings were the result of both the rapid expansion of membership and the development of new and more economical building techniques. Although this third form accommodated many of the same amenities as previous lodge buildings had boasted, the layouts would vary between single-floor designs or ones similar to split-level homes. The newfound popularity in Freemasonry meant new Lodges were chartered throughout the state and these new groups celebrated cornerstone dedications and grand openings.

But with the decline in membership over the last six decades, Masonic lodges have often been burdened by the financial support required to maintain aging and under-occupied buildings. With the consolidation of Lodges across the state, this has left many buildings unoccupied and many communities wondering where the Masons have gone.

Today, the toughs and peaks appear to be leveling out and Freemasonry in New Jersey, and throughout the county, has stabilized. Although many buildings have been lost to sale or demolition, many remain in the hands of dedicated members. The question of reuse remains elusive as the hulking ritual spaces do not easily lend themselves to reuse. Some notable examples of reuse include Hackensack Performing Arts Center, which is housed in a former Masonic Temple, and the Long Branch Masonic Temple, which today is home to Seashore Day Camp & School. In Trenton, hope for preservation emerged when the Historic Trenton Masonic Temple was saved by the Grand Lodge after years of neglect. The imposing 1920s structure has been revitalized and serves once as the Grand Lodge offices with the addition of a museum and library and ample event space. For the local lodge, many resources exist, and groups facing these tough questions should contact local preservation groups and historical societies to learn what opportunities exist within their communities. Much like churches and other community buildings, Masonic lodge buildings play an important role in the cultural heritage of a community. These buildings hold special places not just for the members but also for anyone who has felt the impact of Masonic charity. Although many may be lost, many still remain as testaments to the world's oldest fraternity. As Freemasonry celebrates its tercentennial, only time will tell what will come of New Jersey's Masonic lodges.

A note on nomenclature: when speaking about Freemasonry it is very easy to confuse terminology. For this work, when referring to the "Grand Lodge," the references are to "the Grand Lodge of the Most Ancient and Honorable Society of Free and Accepted Masons for the State of New Jersey." When talking about the fraternity as an organization or philosophy, the form *Mason* or *Masonic* with capital "M" is to be preferred to the lowercase; the latter referencing physical or architectural work in stone. Most importantly, the terms *building, center, lodge,* and *temple* are all used (seemingly interchangeably) in reference to both the organizational unit *and* the physical structures where the groups meet. To prevent confusion, *Lodge* with a capital *L* is to denote the organization unit, while *lodge* in the lowercase is referential to the structure.

One

COLONIAL AND EARLY REPUBLIC NEW JERSEY

For the first several decades of Freemasonry in New Jersey, the craft met in rented spaces in taverns and inns. These spaces proved to be conveniently located, and the availability of food and drink (sometimes even served during meetings) would have added to the fraternal spirit of Masonic events. It would not be until after the establishment of the Grand Lodge of New Jersey that Freemasons in the state would have the first purposed built meeting spaces. Yet even these early structures often contained spaces open to the public or in support of Masonic-led charitable causes.

Over the ensuing centuries, however, only a few buildings remain from the pre–Morgan Affair Era. As for the taverns and inns, the spaces would have been both loud and undecorated. With a bustling business below and with food and drinks provided for travel-weary members, meetings in the Colonial period were very different from the somber and serious affairs they became by the 19th century. The best glimpse into what one of these meetings would have looked like survives in painter John Ward Dunsmore's *The Petition* (1926). Furnished with tables and chairs with a makeshift altar at the center, the limit of decorations may included a trestle board or other symbols drawn in chalk on the floorboards.

But exceptions did occur: a few Lodges built a handful of early lodge buildings. These earliest Masonic structures were largely indistinct and in a vernacular architectural style. In terms of size, the buildings were characteristically small, containing the pure essentials of a lodge room and collation room.

Very few buildings from this period of Masonic history survive, and few records remain that can verify the exact locations of Masonic meetings held in taverns and inns. This lack of records and the sometimes-cloudy memory of Lodges and their histories means that it is impossible to map out all the earliest meeting places. These ensuing pages provide a flavor of the fraternity's earliest days.

1793 OLD MASONIC TEMPLE TRENTON N.J.

Perhaps the most well-known Masonic building among New Jersey Freemasons is the Old Masonic Temple in Trenton. Built in 1793, the two-story five-bay stone structure was the first purpose-built Masonic temple in the state. Trenton Lodge No. 5 had been founded in 1789, and the members had previously met at each other's homes or in local taverns. Mark Thompson donated a plot of land along Front and Barrack Street (known now as Willow Street) to the Lodge for the construction of a building. On the second floor of the building, a lodge room spans the length and width of the space. (Courtesy of the Collection of Erich Morgan Huhn.)

OLD MASONIC TEMPLE TRENTON N.J. 1793

For a brief period in the 1830s, the members of Trenton Lodge No. 5 offered the space to be used as a free school, purportedly the first of its kind in the state. By the 1860s, the Lodge had outgrown the building, and an addition briefly alleviated some of the stress. The building was sold in 1868 and served as a series of shops until it was bought back in 1915. The small building was of little use to the burgeoning fraternity, but antiquarian spirits led to the building being moved to the corner of Barrack and Lafayette Streets. After being moved, the building was extensively restored, and new stonework was needed on some of the original walls. The building reopened as a museum with the intent to display objects of Colonial Masonic history, although the lack of Colonial-era Masonic objects led to the expansion of the museum's interpretation. (Courtesy of the Grand Lodge of New Jersey, 1915.)

The Lodge Room in the Old Masonic Temple, Trenton, has been preserved to its appearance at the time of the building's completion in the 1790s. Simple wooden furniture decorated the room, and still does. Lodges in New Jersey can organize with the Grand Lodge to meet in the old Lodge Room and continue the traditions of Masonic rituals. The ceiling is decorated with stars, the moon, and the sun in reference to points of Masonic ritual. The niche in the "East" of the room has the chair for the Worshipful Master of the Lodge. While the simple ornamentation presents a plain atmosphere, the 18th-century Freemason would have been impressed with the detailing. Masonic lodge rooms would have looked much like this one throughout the 18th and early 19th centuries. (Courtesy of the Library of Congress.)

Although the museum exhibit no longer exists, the building continues to educate the public, serving as the Greater Trenton Visitor Center. The Old Temple is listed as a contributing property to the State House Historic District in both the State and National Register of Historic Places. The Old and New Masonic Temple are part of the Historic Trenton Masonic Temple, a 501c(3) nonprofit organized to preserve both Trenton temples. (Courtesy of the Collection of Erich Morgan Huhn.)

This postcard of the Newark Academy building shows the school's original building. With education and enlightenment as key tenets of Freemasonry, it is not surprising that the fraternity was once a major contributor to educational efforts throughout the state. The third floor of the building was owned and occupied by a Masonic Lodge and fitted with a lodge room. (Courtesy of the Collection of Erich Morgan Huhn.)

The Petition (1926), by John Ward Dunsmore, depicts one of the most important meetings in American Masonic history. Over the winter of 1779–1780, brothers serving in the Continental Army encamped in Morristown met to discuss the future of Freemasonry in the rebellious colonies. The resulting Morristown Convention led to calls for the creation of a Grand Lodge to administer the Craft throughout the new nation. George Washington was rumored to be the

favorite candidate for "Supreme Grand Master." The ensuing petition, which was sent to the various Provincial Grand Lodges, did not gain traction, and the idea ultimately failed. In the following decade, new Grand Lodges were established, and Provincial Grand Lodges declared themselves independent. (Courtesy of New York Historical Society.)

Munn Tavern, on Valley Road in Montclair, was built by Joseph Munn, who opened a tavern here in the first decade of the 19th century. The tavern became popular and Masonic meetings occurred in the public rooms. Bloomfield Lodge, named after Continental Army major and governor Joseph Bloomfield, was supposedly founded in the tavern. The building is now a private residence. (Courtesy of the Library of Congress.)

Built around 1740, Three Tun Tavern was operated by Samuel Briant in Mt. Holly. In 1805, the tavern became the home of a Masonic Lodge, likely Mount Holly Lodge, and changed names to Square and Compass Tavern. By the 1820s, the name had changed again, likely signaling the end of Masonic patronage. The building survives and is now a restaurant. (Courtesy of the Library of Congress.)

Although the postcard below claims Washington Lodge No. 9 as the oldest Masonic Hall in the state, no evidence exists to corroborate the claim. Washington Lodge No. 9, which has since consolidated to form Navesink Lodge No. 9, was established as Washington Lodge No. 34. In the aftermath of the Morgan Affair, many Lodges were renumbered, at which time Washington Lodge No. 34 became No. 9 and moved to Eatontown. The Masonic Hall is still intact, including the addition shown in the postcard. Although the beautiful lancet windows and simple Gothic revival styling has been changed, the building is recognizable driving along Broad Street. The building was locally designated in the Monmouth County Historic Sites Inventory. (Above, courtesy of the Grand Lodge of New Jersey, 1916; below, courtesy of the Collection of Erich Morgan Huhn.)

OLDEST MASONIC HALL IN N. J., ERECTED 1822, REMODELLED 1924.

Brearley Lodge No. 9 was warranted by the Grand Lodge in 1791 and has met in Bridgeton ever since. After the Morgan Affair, the Lodge was renumbered as No. 2. "Old Brearley," their building on Bank Street, is one of the oldest Masonic structures in the state and is a contributing resource on the National Register of Historic Places. (Courtesy of the Grand Lodge of New Jersey, 1919.)

Cincinnati Lodge No. 17 was warranted in 1803 and likely met at members' homes in Montville. It is believed that by 1806, the Lodge moved and took up spaces at the meetinghouse (since demolished) of the Presbyterian church in Whippany. The Lodge continued to meet in Whippany until it was moved to Morristown and renumbered as Cincinnati Lodge No. 3 in 1844. (Courtesy of Cincinnati Lodge No. 3.)

Two

19th-Century Mixed-Use Lodge Buildings

After the doldrums of the Morgan Affair had ended Freemasonry (and fraternalism throughout the country) saw unprecedented growth, particularly after the Civil War through the early 20th century. As the organization grew in membership, Lodges were formed throughout the state. Like in the Colonial, Early Republic, and Morgan Affair periods, these earliest Lodges often met in local taverns or inns, although sentiment was quickly changing. In a country absorbed in the ideas of temperance and revivalism, the sacrilegious surroundings of a tavern or inn were quickly replaced by the trappings of statelier (and exclusively Masonic) spaces.

At the same time, other fraternal organizations saw a boost in membership and faced similar problems. Older fraternal organizations like the Odd Fellows (established in England in the 1730s and in America in the early 1800s) managed a handful of buildings, as did the Freemasons, at this point. New organizations like the United Order of Mechanics and the Sons of Temperance sought physical spaces for themselves as well. The most common answer to the general lack of meeting space was to share buildings and spaces, and many Masonic Lodges met within Odd Fellows Halls and at other fraternal buildings. Conversely, many Masonic Lodges rented out spaces to other fraternal groups. Ultimately, this meant that Masonic and fraternal spaces began to develop into distinct structures within communities. While previously Freemasons met anywhere they could find space, the newly increased demand allowed for the development of distinct fraternal buildings. Yet in the mid- and late 19th century these nascent local Lodges did not have the capital or endowments to support a building exclusively for Masonic use.

As a result, the buildings presented in this chapter show a period of "mixed-use" lodges that became popular. This second form of Masonic lodge was typically found within the main streets of towns and was dominated by unassuming architecture. The plans generally show first-floor elevation occupied by retail space with the possibility for offices on the second floors with the rest of the building devoted to a lodge room and collation room.

The Greenewald Building served a myriad of purposes. Built on Main Street in Moorestown, the building was home to Moorestown Lodge No. 158 (warranted 1887), an Odd Fellows Lodge, a post office, and countless stores in between. In 1916, the Masons erected a new building next door that also included storefronts and was used by the local Odd Fellows. Both buildings have survived. (Courtesy of the Collection of Erich Morgan Huhn.)

This building along Main Street in Orange shows a mixed-use Odd Fellow's Hall where Masonic groups met. Two signs read "Temple of Honor" and "IOOF," and a sign above reads "OUAM" (Order of United American Mechanics). Both Union Lodge No. 11 and Corinthian Lodge No. 57 met in this building before finishing their own temple shown on pages 28 and 29. (Courtesy of the Newark Public Library.)

Masonic
Temple,
Bordentown,
N. J.

MOVING PICTURES

The Masonic Temple in Bordentown was originally Bordentown Hall. Built by the Bordentown Hall Association (BHA) in the 1850s, the building was to serve as a community center, meetinghouse, and offices all with retail on the first floor. Within a year of being established in 1854, Mt. Moriah Lodge No. 28 moved into the third floor of the building. The lodge paid an annual rent of $62.50 and spent an additional $228.14 on furniture and decorations for their rooms. Over the next seven decades, the building would be run by the Bordentown Hall Association and see a variety of businesses occupying the lower floors, including a "Moving Pictures" business, as seen on the marquee. By the 1920s, Mt. Moriah Lodge purchased the remaining stock in the BHA and therefore owned the building outright. While the first-floor storefronts have been removed and the façade has been redone in a Colonial Revival, the building is listed as a contributing resource in the National Register's Bordentown Historic District. (Courtesy of the Collection of Erich Morgan Huhn.)

The Lambertville Masonic Temple, built for Amwell Lodge No. 13 (now No. 12) in the 1870s, was designed by Samuel Sloan. The building housed space for the fraternity along with the first public library, city hall offices, a bank, and countless other commercial ventures. The building today retains much of the original character and is a contributing resource to the National Register historic district. (Courtesy of the Collection of Erich Morgan Huhn.)

The Camden Masonic Temple, long since demolished, was one of several Masonic buildings that have since been lost to the wrecking ball in Camden. This building, formerly on Market Street, was also the home to the Temple Theater and was one of the first stage theaters in the city when it opened in 1892. (Courtesy of the Collection of Erich Morgan Huhn.)

Another building lost to history is the Mount Holly Masonic Temple. Built by Mount Holly Lodge No. 14 in 1891. The building served as a Masonic Temple, post office, and retail space. After a foreclosure saw the building change owners, the Freemasons continued to rent the space until a fire in 1925 gutted the building. (Courtesy of the Collection of Erich Morgan Huhn.)

Masonic Temple, Mount Holly, N. J.

H. L. KEELER, PHOTOGRAPHER, MOUNT HOLLY, N. J.

No 10—Masonic Temple, Union Hill, N. J.

This Masonic Temple in Union Hill (now part of Union City) is a perfect example of the mixed-use 19th-century form. Without any clear markings on the exterior, this building would blend in with other commercial storefronts. While the building is likely long since demolished, the blend of architectural details from the fenestration, tower, and terra-cotta detailing make this an interesting lodge. (Courtesy of the Collection of Erich Morgan Huhn.)

MASONIC TEMPLE, ORANGE, N. J.

The Masonic Temple on Main Street in Orange is one of a handful of the impressive mixed-use Masonic lodge buildings from before the turn of the 19th century. Still, without any obviously Masonic symbolism on the façade, the building is one of the more elaborate from this period. Done in an eclectic Queen Anne style the building is clad in bright red brick and terra-cotta ornamentation. Over the course of the building's association with the Freemasons, several Lodges have met in the structure. (Both, courtesy of the Collection of Erich Morgan Huhn.)

Post Office and Masonic Building, Orange, N. J.

28

"CENTENNIAL OF THE ORANGES, N.J."
1504 Masonic Building and Post Office, Main St.
Photo by F. P. Jewett.

Shown here draped in patriotic bunting, the "Masonic Building" on Main Street in Orange appears decorated for a parade. The building still stands, although major alterations have left the first-floor storefronts unrecognizable. Along with being home to Masonic activity, the building had storefronts and served as the local post office for a period. Both Union Lodge No. 21 and Corinthian Lodge No. 57 met in the building before merging and ultimately becoming Livingston Lodge No. 11. As membership grew in through the early 20th century, this style of the mixed-use building began to fall from favor, although Lodges continued to meet in this and other buildings like it. One of the obvious benefits to these historic buildings is the rental income available from retail or office space, a source of revenue many Lodges today wish they could accommodate. (Courtesy of the Collection of Erich Morgan Huhn.)

Masonic Temple, Trenton, N. J.

The Masonic temple in Trenton at the corner of State and Warren Streets has since been demolished but presents one of the greatest examples of 19th-century mixed-use Masonic lodge buildings in the state. This "Second" Masonic temple was built between 1884 and 1885. Like many Masonic temples and buildings, the construction and management were organized through a stock company where members (and ultimately the public) were able to own stock in the building. The building became home to several Lodges and included space for Royal Arch, Knights Templar, and Shriner organizations, all appendant "related" Masonic organizations. However, the Trenton Banking Company slowly gained a controlling stake of the building and demolished the structure to build a new main office. (Courtesy of the Collection of Erich Morgan Huhn.)

Masonic Temple, Trenton, N. J.

Trenton May 16. 1906

Education was always an important part of Masonic philosophy and charity. Just as with the Newark Academy and the "Old" Masonic Temple in Trenton, the Second Masonic temple in Trenton became home to an educational institution. The building was, as touted in this advertisement, "without a doubt, one of the finest structures in the State of New Jersey." Beyond the building's Masonic and retail tenants, Trenton Business College (later Rider Business College and eventually Rider University) enjoyed ample space for lecture rooms, a library, and even a gymnasium on the fourth floor. Andrew Jackson Rider, the "Principal and Proprietor" of Trenton Business College, was a Freemason and became well known as the "Cranberry King of New Jersey" resulting from his promotion of the cranberry industry. Today, very little is remembered of the Second Masonic temple in Trenton or Rider University's connection with New Jersey Freemasonry. (Courtesy of the Newark Public Library.)

These two photographs show a rare view of the Lodge Room of Cincinnati Lodge No. 3 in a mixed-use building the Lodge rented through the late 19th century. As the ritualistic center of Masonic activity, this room played an important role as the symbolic Temple of King Solomon. The photograph above shows the "East," from where the Worshipful Master of the Lodge would lead meetings. By the end of the 19th century, many companies were selling not just costumes and jewelry to be used during Lodge meetings but also full furniture suites. The set shown here includes officer and station chairs, pedestals, tapers, and an altar. More elaborate than the public rooms of a tavern or the simple lodge rooms of earlier lodges, consumerism meant Masonic rituals could be more easily displayed. (Courtesy of Cincinnati Lodge No. 3.)

Three

20TH-CENTURY MIXED-USE LODGE BUILDINGS

Although with the turn of the century the use of mixed-use design for Masonic lodge buildings had declined, several new buildings of this style were built through the end of the Golden Age of Fraternalism. This period of expanded growth saw the popularity of Freemasonry expand, resulting in new Lodges being formed in a rapidly growing urban/suburban New Jersey.

Much like the mixed-use buildings of the 19th century, the 20th-century counterparts were designed with at least two floors. While the first floors were rented to provide Lodges with a steady income, the upper floors were reserved for the use of the Masonic and fraternal bodies meeting in the lodge. Unlike the 19th-century forms, however, the 20th-century mixed-use buildings would be designed with a much more distinct and stately architectural style. Where once unassuming and innocuous structures were built, the 20th-century forms attempted rather to impose the power and influence of the growing fraternity.

Drawing references from classical architecture, many of these late mixed-use Masonic Lodge buildings came more directly to represent the "temples" they symbolized within Masonic ritual. Columns, pilasters, cornices, and pediments, which had been incorporated as subtle details in earlier mixed-use lodge buildings, became key architectural features of these new buildings in an attempt to link the fraternity to the ancient and noble past referenced in Masonic origin myths. This attempt to historicize the physical structures ran parallel to the popularity of Classical and Colonial Revival architectural styles that sought to impress the power and dignity of an organization through architectural design.

As will be shown in the upcoming chapters, the Classical and Colonial Revival styles became popular architectural motifs for Masonic lodge buildings for decades to come yet other styles remained. The examples in this chapter show some of the last mixed-use forms built in the state as the fraternity, emboldened by large membership dues and participation, shifted to construct purpose-built Masonic temples.

This Masonic Hall, at the intersections of Clinton, Springfield, Union, and Myrtle Avenues in Irvington, was home to several Lodges. Franklin Lodge No. 10 and Vehslage Lodge No. 225 both met in the building. In the later 20th century, both Lodges moved out, and the building's façade, here obscured by patriotic bunting, was replaced with a more modern design. (Courtesy of the Newark Public Library.)

This temple, home to Copestone Lodge No. 147, is located along Kearny Avenue in the business district of Kearny. The building, erected in 1916, shows an early example as Masonic Lodges started implementing more classical design into their buildings. The Lodge is still active and continues to use the building, which has two storefronts on the first floor. (Courtesy of the Grand Lodge of New Jersey, 1918.)

Clinton Hill Lodge No. 209 built this three-story mixed-use building in the 1920s along Clinton Avenue in Newark. Designed by Strombach & Mertens, the building cost $125,000 and featured a two-story colonnade. Although several Lodges called the building home, the Freemasons sold the building in the late-20th century, and nothing of the original façade remains. (Courtesy of the Grand Lodge of New Jersey, 1923.)

The Masonic Temple on Park Avenue and Seventh Street in Plainfield represents one of the more imposing implementations of Masonic historicist design. Built in 1927, the building is home to Jerusalem Lodge No. 26. The ionic pilasters support an entablature which features a square and compass ornamented with festoon and medallions. (Courtesy of the Grand Lodge of New Jersey, 1929.)

The Masonic Building along East Landis Avenue in Vineland represents one of the most impressive of the 20th-century mixed-use form. Erected in the 1920s as a home for Vineland Lodge No. 69, the building is done in the typical Colonial Revival style. The five-bay façade is divided by a series of four simple pilasters along the upper two floors while the first floor is dominated by a shopfront. The decorative features along the entablature are dominated by festoon and the central three balconettes feature the Masonic square and compass motif inside wreaths. Although this is no longer a Masonic Lodge building, much of the architectural details, apart from the first-floor elevation, has been retained during the conversion into a fully commercial property. (Courtesy of the Grand Lodge of New Jersey, 1925.)

Masonic Hall
Nutley N.J.

Wm. A. LAMBERT
Architect

The two Masonic lodges shown here present aberrations from the typical 20th-century mixed-use form. The Masonic Hall on Franklin Avenue in Nutley was built by Nutley Lodge No. 167 and designed by William A. Lambert, an architect noted for his residential designs which dominate the town. Atypical of Lambert's residential work, the Masonic Hall is done in brick and masonry with three courses and bay window shopfronts along the first floor. The photograph below, of Edgemont Lodge in Montclair, presents a more modern approach to lodge architecture. Built in 1926, the building is done in a modern style more typical of commercial buildings built between 1920 and 1940s. Both buildings remain and have suffered only minor alterations. (Above, Courtesy of the Newark Public Library; below, courtesy of the Collection of Erich Morgan Huhn.)

EDGEMONT LODGE
MONTCLAIR N.J.

Four

ADAPTIVE REUSE

As seen in the previous chapters, Masonic buildings did not vary significantly for the first 100 years in New Jersey. Although for the earliest stages inns, taverns, and makeshift arrangements dominated Lodge existence, by the 19th and early 20th centuries, the demand required expanded (and often dedicated) space for Masonic ritual. As membership grew in the early 20th century, Lodges that were not interested in building new structures (even if that meant possible rental income) looked to the existing building stock to address the needs of the growing Craft.

In the field of historic preservation, the "conversion" of a structure from one purpose to another is referred to as adaptive reuse. Although this term (and the entire field of historic preservation) did not emerge until the 1960s, the Freemasons have purchased buildings, often of historic nature, and repurposed the structures for new life as Masonic lodges. The buildings Freemasons have adapted range from homes and local community clubs to massive churches.

Individual homes, often historic features in the community, were sometimes bought by the Freemasons. With a bit of imagination, Lodges remodeled original residential structures to provide the spaces needed to conduct ceremony and host events. Clubs presented a few cases of adaptive reuse for the Masons of New Jersey, with large buildings and space for events the structures were a natural fit. What appears to be the most popular of structure for adaptive reuse seems to have been churches. As congregations ebbed and waned church buildings were often left abandoned, but to the Freemasons, these buildings presented a convenient new home with inspiring architecture and ample space for ceremony.

This chapter presents a few of the many cases of adaptive reuse that the Freemasons have done over the years. The irony exists that, since the decline in membership and the consolidation of so many Lodge organizations, many of the structures shown throughout this book, which were built as Masonic Lodge buildings themselves, have been repurposed and adapted to serve new lives.

The need for large, uninterrupted spaces to conduct rituals and ceremony in means that the small and divided spaces found in residential structures would leave Masonic Lodges wanting. By adding additions off the back to house the ritual spaces, Lodges provided ample room for ceremony while also being able to provide recreational space. The Masonic Temple in Ramsey, shown above, actually burnt down in the 1960s, and the members of Fortitude Lodge rebuilt their Masonic home in a similar form. The members of Excelsior Lodge No. 54, in Salem, took the Gothic Revival Morris Hall House and converted the building in 1959 with the addition off the rear. The Morris Hall House, while extant, no longer serves as a Masonic temple. (Above, courtesy of the Grand Lodge of New Jersey, 1933; below, courtesy of the Grand Lodge of New Jersey, 1960.)

This classic late-19th-century brick home, with a large porch, turret, and gabled roofs, shows an addition off the rear, which would likely have housed Masonic ceremonial space. This Masonic Temple was at the corner of Third and Broad Street in Newark before being demolished and was home to Delta Lodge No. 232. (Courtesy of the Grand Lodge of New Jersey, 1922.)

The Masonic Temple of Keyport, at the corner of Osborn Street and Third Avenue, was built by Thomas Arrowsmith in the 1850s. The home would have been an impressive residence for the sea captain in the bustling port town. Caesarea Lodge No. 64 moved into the building in the first half of the 20th century. (Courtesy of the Grand Lodge of New Jersey, 1930.)

The Jacob W. Van Winkle House, built in 1798, served as a residence until the Masonic Club of Lyndhurst purchased the property in 1921. The home would have been built as a one-room structure, with expansions added in the 19th century. The building is individually listed on the National Register of Historic Places. (Courtesy of the Meadowlands Museum.)

The Warren House on Front Street in Belvidere has a long history of adaptive reuse. Built in 1838 by Maj. Benjamin Depue, the home was used as a hotel through the 19th century. After a devastating fire, the building was purchased and converted into a Masonic lodge by the members of Warren Lodge No. 13. The building is a contributing asset to the Belvidere Historic District. (Courtesy of the Collection of Erich Morgan Huhn.)

The Aycrigg Mansion, along Temple Place in Passaic, was built in 1848 as the home for wealthy physician and former congressman John Bancker Aycrigg. Although the home served as a residence for some 50 years, it served as the Passaic Collegiate School briefly before becoming a Masonic temple in 1908. While the Masonic temple, the Aycrigg Mansion was home to several Masonic Lodges, including Lessing Lodge No. 189 which conducted all rituals and ceremonies in German until a statewide ban required English only ritual in 1919. Equity Lodge No. 257 was formed at this Masonic temple in 1925 as an ethnically Jewish Lodge. The building survives and, today, serves as a Jewish school not associated with the Freemasons. The building is on the National Register of Historic Places. (Above, courtesy of the Grand Lodge of New Jersey, 1916; below, courtesy of the Library of Congress.)

Clubhouses also made convenient adaptive Masonic lodge buildings. This building on Bergen Avenue in Jersey City, which once housed Bergen Lodge No. 47, was originally built by a neighborhood association to serve as a private, members-only library. The building served a myriad of other purposes over the years and became known as the Bergen Lyceum. After the Freemasons left the building, it was given new life as the home to a succession of churches. Today, the building is listed as a contributing resource for the West Bergen–East Lincoln Park Historic District on the National Register. (Courtesy of the Grand Lodge of New Jersey, 1915.)

The Masonic Temple shown here, on Cooper Avenue in Upper Montclair, presents a typical Masonic mystery. The building is labeled on this postcard as the Masonic Temple, but records show that Mountain Lodge No. 214 met next door at the Commonwealth Club. While it is likely that the Freemasons may have used the space shown above, the irony is that the building has long served as home to the Women's Club of Upper Montclair. (Courtesy of the Collection of Erich Morgan Huhn.)

The Masonic Temple in Metuchen on Middlesex Avenue was originally built as the home of the Metuchen Club. In the 1920s, Mt. Zion Lodge No. 135 purchased the building and adapted the structure for Masonic uses. The building is still used by Mt. Zion Lodge and is listed as a contributing resource on a National Register historic district. (Courtesy of the Collection of Erich Morgan Huhn.)

MASONIC TEMPLE, LITTLE FALLS, N.J.

The Masonic temple shown here, on Lincoln Avenue in Little Falls, presents one of the more unique conversions. The building was originally built for the Mack Molding Company but was purchased by Little Falls Lodge No. 263 in 1931. This building is most likely the only conversion of an industrial building to Masonic lodge in the state. (Courtesy of the Collection of Erich Morgan Huhn.)

Before becoming the home to Kane Lodge No. 55, this building served as the home to the First Protestant Church. The large ceremonial spaces and inspiring architecture found in 19th-century churches meant shifting from church to Masonic lodge was easy. Kane Lodge was based out of this building through the 1970s, when many Masonic Lodges moved out of Newark and other urban areas. (Courtesy of the Newark Public Library.)

The Masonic Temple in Madison, built in 1824 as a Presbyterian church, presents a typical Early Republic brick church building. The simple three-bay design with a tall steeple is done in the Federal style and has been carefully maintained by Madison Lodge No. 93. In 1931, when Madison Lodge moved into the building, the understanding was that the exterior of the building should be preserved and only a small kitchen addition was put off the rear. Part of the renovations undertaken in the 1930s included the closing off a second-floor balcony that split the former nave into a lodge room and collation room. In 2008, in recognition for the hard work the Lodge had done to preserve their building, the structure was listed in the National Register and is currently the only individually listed Masonic temple in New Jersey. (Courtesy of the Grand Lodge of New Jersey, 1930.)

Livingston Lodge No. 289 met at this location, the former Olivet Presbyterian Chapel on Route 10 and Old Road in Livingston, for just over 50 years. The chapel was built in 1892 and served the small congregation through to 1950. Livingston Lodge No. 289 has since merged and moved out of the building, ironically into a former Grange Hall. (Courtesy of the Newark Public Library.)

This former church turned Masonic temple presents another Masonic mystery. Listed in the Grand Lodge *Proceedings*, the building was likely home to Union Lodge No. 19, which would have met in the building through the 1970s. A Masonic Temple Association was formed in New Brunswick and likely purchased the building with a consortium of Masonic Lodges. The building has since been demolished. (Courtesy of the Grand Lodge of New Jersey, 1916.)

The First Italian Presbyterian Church, shown here after being converted to serve as the lodge for Newark Lodge No. 7 around 1914, was formerly on Plane Street (now University Avenue) in Newark. The building's rusticated stonework and small windows give the structure the appearance of a medieval chapel, although it was likely built in the later 19th century. (Courtesy of the Grand Lodge of New Jersey, 1919.)

The Masonic temple in Cedar Grove on Pompton Avenue was originally part of St. David's Episcopal Church. The Freemasons of Cedar Lodge No. 275 purchased the building in 1936 and converted the space to serve as a Masonic Temple. The building still stands, but alterations have made the structure hardly recognizable, and it now serves as a commercial property. (Courtesy of the Collection of Erich Morgan Huhn.)

One of the most impressive instances of adaptive reuse found among New Jersey Masonic Lodges was that of the Masonic temple in Hackensack. Built in 1849 as the First Methodist Church, Pioneer Lodge No. 70 purchased and converted the property to Masonic use in the late 19th century. By the 2000s, the Freemasons no longer required such a large space, and in 2011, the City of Hackensack purchased the building to be converted into a performing arts center. Today, the 170-year-old church lives on as the Hackensack Performing Arts Center and serves the community in a new capacity. For the field of historic preservation, adaptive reuse presents an important (and often economic and environmental) tool to prevent the loss of important pieces of cultural heritage. By saving the building, the memories of both the congregation and the brothers who have met here live on. (Courtesy of the Grand Lodge of New Jersey, 1921.)

Five

GOLDEN AGE

By the early 20th century, Masonic Lodges had enjoyed a relatively steady increase in membership and fortunes for over five decades. At the same time, the increasing development of New Jersey meant that once rural and quiet communities became bustling suburban commuter enclaves. As towns developed and grew, so did Masonic Lodges. This period, referred to as the Golden Age of Fraternalism, saw the construction of some of the most iconic and interesting Masonic Lodge buildings in the state.

As evident in the ensuing pages, the architectural styles invoked in the new form of single-purposed Masonic temples ranged from Classical to contemporary depending on the tastes and ambitions of individual Lodges. In smaller towns, Lodges built new buildings in more appropriate vernacular styles while Lodges in emerging suburbs hired architects to build elaborate new temples.

Along with the costs of construction and hiring architects, the maintenance of these new Temples put considerable strain on local Lodges. To fund and manage this new form of Masonic Temple, temple associations were formed throughout the state. These corporations were formed essentially as holding companies which were owned (most commonly) by the Masonic Lodge itself. By forming these corporations, Masonic Lodges were able to issue bonds and raise funds to afford the often-expensive endeavors of building a new home. Often, temple associations would be composed of officers representing the several Masonic organizations which would call the new lodge home. From blue lodges to commanderies and chapters, temple associations were a convenient means to organize the maintenance of the new buildings.

The buildings created by the Freemasons from the first half of the 20th century show not only the growing influence of the fraternity, but also the growing diversity as other "Masonic" groups band together literally under one roof. The large columns and imposing façades from this period provide a physical and constructed symbol of the growing fraternity. Today, many of these buildings have survived. While some have passed from the hands that built them, many remain and harken back to a period of impressive growth and investment.

The Masonic Temple of Tuckahoe presents a simple example of the Classical Revival architectural style, which became popular through the first half of the 20th century. Built for Star Lodge No. 65, the building at the corner of Mt. Pleasant Road and State Route 50 is a contributing resource to the North and South Tuckahoe Historic District. (Courtesy of the Grand Lodge of New Jersey, 1929.)

Egg Harbor City's Masonic Temple, built around 1900, was home to Hiram T. Dewey Lodge No. 226. The building, along Philadelphia Avenue, is done in a simplified Colonial Revival style popular at the time, featuring pilasters and columns. The simplified styling presents a cost-effective, yet stylish, lodge building. (Courtesy of the Grand Lodge of New Jersey, 1933.)

The former Masonic Temple on Knox Avenue in Cliffside Park is another example of a low-key Colonial Revival local Masonic lodge. The simple ornamentation is enhanced by English bond brickwork was likely built within the first two decades of the 20th century. Ironically, after Whitehead Lodge No. 184 vacated the building, it became home to the Turkish American Religious Federation. (Courtesy of the Collection of Erich Morgan Huhn.)

The Masonic Temple, shown here along Garden Street in Mount Holly, was built in 1931 for Mount Holly Lodge No. 14. After the previous building had burnt down in 1925, the Lodge purchased the plot along Garden Street in 1926. The building was designed by Philadelphia architect J. Fletcher Street and cost nearly $40,000 to build. (Courtesy of the Grand Lodge of New Jersey, 1931.)

The Masonic Temple, built by Lafayette Lodge No. 27 in Rahway, was a project 20 years in the making. Lafayette Lodge had a long history in the town, established in 1824 and named after the Marquis de Lafayette, who had been on a celebrated American tour when the Lodge was formed. Initially, the Lodge met in several rented spaces. (Courtesy of the Collection of Erich Morgan Huhn.)

The Lodge purchased the lot on Irving Street in 1904, but the cornerstone was not laid until 1924. Seymour Williams, a prominent local architect, was engaged to design the building and included space for a "Craftsmen's Club," with an entrance on the right. For a time, the building also housed municipal offices. (Courtesy of the Grand Lodge of New Jersey, 1925.)

The Long Branch Masonic Temple on Broadway was built in 1925 for Long Branch Lodge No. 78. Long Branch Lodge was formed in 1967 and rented space for over 50 years before building the Masonic temple, where the Lodge continued to meet for 55 years. In 1980, the Lodge was consolidated with Abacus Lodge No. 182 of Long Branch and, the next year, consolidated again with George B. Moxley Lodge No. 277 of Fair Haven. The building, with large columns and decorative features, provides an important transition from simpler to more elaborate designs. During World War II, the building was opened by the Freemasons (along with other Masonic lodges in the state) and served as an Army and Navy service center. The building survived the consolidations and has since served as a private school. (Courtesy of the Grand Lodge of New Jersey, 1927.)

This photograph shows the ceremonies at the beginning of construction for the Morristown Masonic Temple. The event reportedly drew 2,000 people and included delegates from the Grand Lodge, Knights Templar (note the man in Templar uniform and chapeau in the left foreground), and local and state officials. Events like these were popular in the period and would have included the dedication of the cornerstone, a procession through town, speeches, and most likely a dinner or other entertainment. The actual cornerstone dedication is one of the few Masonic ceremonies that can be done with the public present and includes anointing the cornerstone of any building with wine, corn, and oil. Not just limited to Masonic buildings, the Freemasons have dedicated cornerstones of countless buildings. (Courtesy of the North Jersey History and Genealogy Center.)

The Morristown Masonic Center, built in 1930, was one of the earliest principal works of Paul W. Drake, FAIA (Fellow of the American Institute of Architects). The building was planned to serve several organizations and was owned by the Morristown Masonic Temple Association. The temple association was controlled by a board of representatives from each of the four organizations that funded and erected the building, including two blue lodges, a Knights Templar commander, and a Royal Arch Masons chapter. At a cost of just over $80,000, the building was touted by New Jersey governor (and Freemason) A. Harry Moore as "a symbol of Freemasonry" at his dedication speech. Done in the Colonial Revival style, the building includes a lodge room with space for over 100 members. The altar and officer chairs were brought from an earlier building on Washington Avenue (page 32). Visiting Cincinnati Lodge No. 3, the only remaining of the four groups that built the building, the lodge room looks almost identical to how it is pictured below. (Both, courtesy of the North Jersey History and Genealogy Center.)

Although the original plans by Drake included a second-floor lounge, the temple association went with a more scaled-back design, perhaps in reaction to the decline in the stock market, which occurred just as building was about to begin. With wood trim, built-in bookcases, and a fireplace, this parlor remains largely intact from its appearance on the opening day in this photograph. (Courtesy of the North Jersey History and Genealogy Center.)

By this time, and in the form of purpose-built Masonic lodges, the buildings almost universally contain a collation room, or banquet hall, directly underneath the lodge room. Almost as important as the ritual itself, holding a collation after a meeting still forms an important part of Masonic traditions. Fundraising dinners and events are often held in these rooms to help promote the Lodge and charitable causes. (Courtesy of the North Jersey History and Genealogy Center.)

The Haddonfield Masonic Temple (above) along East Kings Highway and the Masonic Temple of Union City (below) both present Classical Revival styling for Masonic lodges. Both built in the early 1920s, the large columns and pediments liken the buildings to Greek or Roman temples. Within initiation rituals, the orders of classical architecture, and the inspiring buildings would have served as testaments to the Crafts influence and history. Rising Sun Lodge No. 15 built the Haddonfield Masonic temple and continues to meet in the building, which is within the National Register Historic District. The Union City Temple was built for Doric Lodge No. 86, which merged in the 1980s and moved out to Secaucus. The building was demolished to make way for a community pool. (Above, courtesy of the Collection of Erich Morgan Huhn; below, courtesy of the Grand Lodge of New Jersey, 1926.)

The Masonic Temple of Hawthorne was built in the 1920s for Hawthorne Lodge No. 212 along Lafayette Avenue. Built in the 1920s, the building takes a more modern interpretation on the Classical styles, with pilasters and a prominent entablature that is typical of commercial interpretations of the style. Although Hawthorne Lodge No. 212 merged with Fortitude Lodge No. 100 in 1988, the building survived and is now a medical office. (Courtesy of the Grand Lodge of New Jersey, 1927.)

The Park Ridge Masonic Temple along Kinderkamack Road and the Hawthorne Masonic Temple are both examples of a transition between the strict Classical Revival found on the opposite page and more modern interpretations. Also built in the 1920s, the Park Ridge Masonic Temple was home to Friendship Lodge No. 102, which merged and still meets in the building. (Courtesy of the Collection of Erich Morgan Huhn.)

The Masonic Temples of South Amboy (above) and Penns Grove (below) both present similar examples of more modern designs for Masonic lodges. In South Amboy, the former lodge on Main Street was built for St. Stephen's Lodge No. 6, which has since moved out of the building. The lodge in Penns Grove along West Main Street was built for Penns Grove Lodge No. 162 and used through the 1990s before the Lodge merged and moved out. The Penns Grove Temple is particularly interesting, with the large square form and simple designs invoking an almost Egyptianesque feel that was very popular in the 1920s. Neither buildings are currently owned by the Freemasons, and both are vacant. (Above, courtesy of the Grand Lodge of New Jersey, 1925; below, courtesy of the Grand Lodge of New Jersey, 1926.)

Although the previous chapter showcased some examples of lodges that had been adapted from other uses, countless examples survive of lodges themselves being transformed into new lives after the Freemasons leave. The Masonic Temple on Joralemon Street in Belleville was built for Belleville Lodge No. 108 but has since gotten a new life as a Hindu temple. (Courtesy of the Collection of Erich Morgan Huhn.)

The Camden Masonic Temple formerly on Fourth Street was built as the replacement to the older Masonic temple (page 29). The lavish new building was inaugurated with great fanfare. The building's stately columns, however, were demolished in the 1990s after all the Masonic Lodges that had met in the building moved out or merged, many of whom went on to form USS New Jersey Lodge No. 62. (Courtesy of the Grand Lodge of New Jersey, 1915.)

The Masonic Temple of Closter, on Durie Avenue, was built in the 1930s as the home of Alpine Lodge No. 77. The building's stucco façade and radius windows create an almost Mediterranean appearance. Alpine Lodge No. 77 moved out in the 1980s, but the building is still largely intact and has received new life as a Hindu center. (Courtesy of the Grand Lodge of New Jersey, 1932.)

Jersey City's Masonic Temple, built in 1911 on Bergen Avenue, presents a more traditional design with two striking columns dividing the three-story building. By 1915, ten Masonic Lodges listed the building as their home. Although the Freemasons have left, the building has since been converted into a church. (Courtesy of the Grand Lodge of New Jersey, 1915.)

Done in a Gothic style, the Bayonne Masonic Temple on Avenue C was built in 1926 by Bayonne Lodge No. 99. The building was the Lodge's first permanent home and cost approximately $125,000. The façade and fenestration present a building that looks as it was plucked from medieval Europe. (Courtesy of the Grand Lodge of New Jersey, 1927.)

Located abutting the Hudson County Park, the lodge is neatly nestled into a residential neighborhood and has played an important role in the community. The Lodge that currently meets in the building, Peninsula Lodge No. 99, is the result of five merges over the last 50 years. (Courtesy of the Collection of Erich Morgan Huhn.)

The Masonic Temple built by Hope Lodge No. 124 in East Orange has since been demolished but at the time was the summation of nearly 10 years of planning. After purchasing the lots around 1903, it took another seven years of fundraising before the cornerstone was dedicated in 1910. The building, which cost approximately $250,000, included spaces for Masonic activity and appendant body meeting rooms. The building was referred to as the Lyceum and included retail space and a vaudeville theater as early as 1916. The theater was converted from vaudeville to a movie theatre in the 1930s and became known as the Ormont Movie Theatre, all while the Masons still owned and met in the building. The temple was demolished after the Masonic Lodges that had met there moved as urbanization and white flight spread through New Jersey's urban centers. (Courtesy of the Grand Lodge of New Jersey, 1916.)

The Roseville Masonic Temple was built in the Egyptian Revival style for several Masonic Lodges that were meeting in the area. The building, designed by Jordan Green and opened in 1913, was featured in *American Architect & Architecture* in a multipage spread. The ornate façade with decorative brickwork and Egyptian motifs reflects the monumental architectural scale and massing of an ancient temple. Although Masonic rituals claim a connection dating back to the time of the Pharaohs and certain esoteric scholars have made claims supporting this, there is no proof of any Masonic connection. The building was demolished in 1966 to make way for Interstate 280. (Right, courtesy of the Grand Lodge of New Jersey, 1915; below, courtesy of the Newark Public Library.)

The South Amboy Masonic Temple, built on State Street in the 1920s, was designed by Benjamin Goldberger. Built for a consortium of Masonic groups, the building was originally dedicated to Masonic use. The plain, institutional architecture with cast stone entablature and simple brickwork and pilasters, presents a building that largely blends in with the surrounding commercial district of South Amboy. Over the decades, the Masonic groups that had built the structure had consolidated or moved out, and by the 1960s, only Raritan Lodge No. 61 and Prudence Lodge No. 204 remained, and space in the building was converted for rental as offices. In the 1980s, a member sustained injuries after falling down the elevator shaft and sued the Lodges and temple association. This financial setback made its way through the New Jersey court system and dealt a significant blow to the Lodge at a time when membership throughout the state was facing challenges. Although the building survives, the Freemasons have since sold and moved out. (Courtesy of the Grand Lodge of New Jersey, 1924.)

The Masonic temples of Secaucus and Phillipsburg present two variations of modern design. Both completed in the late 1930s, the buildings share similar massing, with large two-story three-bay form punctuated by relatively smaller windows in a simple pattern. The Secaucus Masonic Temple, on Paterson Plank Road, is done in a more modern variegated brick, while the Phillipsburg Temple, on Hillcrest Boulevard, is more restrained and features cast stone entablature and sills. Both buildings reference Art Deco in their cast architrave, form, and decorations. Philipsburg Lodge No. 52 and Secaucus Hudson Lodge No. 72 (the decedent of the Lodge that erected the structure) both still meet in the buildings. (Above, courtesy of the Grand Lodge of New Jersey, 1939; below, Courtesy of the Grand Lodge of New Jersey, 1936.)

The Eagle Lyceum on Hutton Street in Jersey City was home to Eagle Lodge No. 53 and Enterprise Lodge No. 87. The building, with impressive red brickwork and ornamentation, presents an ornate historicist multistory building amid a developing community. The decorative brickwork around the curved second-floor window heads and the cornice work with large central pediment mix architectural styles from the various revivalist styles of the period. The building served a wider audience in the community and was known as the Eagle Lyceum. Eagle Lodge moved out of the building after merging with several others that became Secaucus Hudson Lodge No. 72 (page 69). Enterprise Lodge No. 31, which had previously met in the Jersey City Masonic Temple (page 68), has since moved into the building where they continue to meet. (Courtesy of the Grand Lodge of New Jersey, 1921.)

Azure Lodge No. 129 built the Masonic Temple of Cranford on South Avenue in the 1930s. The building is done in a more traditional Colonial Revival style. The Lodge, which claimed its former building was the world's first electrically lit Masonic lodge, still meets in the building as AzureMasada Lodge No. 22. (Courtesy of the Grand Lodge of New Jersey, 1930.)

The Bogota Masonic Temple, on Palisades Avenue, was built in the 1920s for William F. Burk Lodge No. 230. The large airy windows have since been replaced with modern inserts; alterations like these present an unfortunate reality for historic buildings as they detract from the historical integrity and often cost more in the long run than proper rehab. (Courtesy of the Grand Lodge of New Jersey, 1926.)

The Masonic Temples in Palisades Park (above) and Atlantic Highlands (below) both present smaller and simpler designs for Masonic temples. In Palisades Park, the Masonic temple was built in 1921 for Townley Lodge No. 220 in rubble masonry style. In 1984, the Lodge merged with William F. Burk Lodge No. 230 in Bogota (page 65), and the building has since become an Armenian American Community Center. The Atlantic Highlands Temple, built in 1939 in a vernacular shingle style, is the home of Monmouth Lodge No. 172. Although the Atlantic Highlands Temple has since been covered in vinyl siding, much of the building's simple features remain intact. (Above, courtesy of the Grand Lodge of New Jersey, 1921; below, courtesy of the Grand Lodge of New Jersey, 1939.)

MASONIC TEMPLE,
WESTFIELD, N. J.

Built in 1928, the Westfield Masonic Temple, formerly on Temple Place, was the home to Atlas Lodge No. 125. Atlas Lodge had met in several spaces after being warranted in 1871 before building the Masonic temple. The building's decorative brickwork and Egyptian-styled parapet and medallions present a late example of Egyptian Revival towards the end of the style's popularity. The building was dedicated at a ceremony and parade of 1,000 Masons and included remarks by Governor Moore and other local dignitaries. The building burnt down in February 1970, and the Lodge ultimately rebuilt along Central Avenue (page 96). (Above, courtesy of the Collection of Erich Morgan Huhn, below, courtesy of the Grand Lodge of New Jersey, 1929.)

The Mountain Lakes Masonic Temple was built as the home for Mountain Lakes Lodge No. 258. The entire surrounding community was developed starting in the 1910s by developer Herbert Hapgood. In 1924, as work on the Masonic Temple began, the Belhall Company was formed to take over the development after Hapgood had become embroiled in scandal. The building was done in a style typical of the Hapgood-Belhall designs, with stucco and featuring half-timber in a Craftsman-Tutor style unique to the community. The building forms a contributing resource within the Mountain Lakes Historic District and is one of many original structures from the development of the community in the 1910s and 1920s. In the 1970s, as St. John's Lodge No. 1 in Newark was facing closure, the Lodge moved and merged with Mountain Lakes Lodge No. 258 and is still active under the St. John's name and number. (Courtesy of the Collection of Erich Morgan Huhn.)

Six

GRAND DESIGNS

While the building boom of the first half of the 20th century may have dotted the state with Masonic temples, a few examples stand out. In large cities like Paterson, Elizabeth, Trenton, and Atlantic City, the Masonic groups sought to build lasting monuments to the fraternity. These new, near mega-temples were collaborations between several Masonic Lodges and appendant bodies coming together to raise funds and organize the massive building projects. The resulting buildings present some of the largest and most impressive architectural works completed by the Freemasons in New Jersey.

This new form of "grand design" Masonic temples was centered on multiple lodge rooms, libraries, game rooms, dining rooms, offices, and often, an auditorium. Expensive materials were used and often features marble and granite throughout the building. Hiring prominent architects, these grand Masonic Temples were as much a display about the power and influence of the fraternity as they were an advertising tool to attract interest. As it still does today, membership in a Masonic Lodge opens endless possibilities of social gatherings and events. In the organization's heyday, buildings like these hosted an endless string of activities and events, not just for members of the Lodges but also for appendant bodies and the community.

When these large buildings were planned, they were meant to be used by multiple Lodges. As with the smaller temples, temple associations were formed to organize and fund through bonds the construction of these complexes. After the initial funding for the construction was provided, the upkeep would have been funded through annual fees. Unfortunately, as membership began to decline and white flight shifted the demographics of major New Jersey cities, the viability of these large buildings was called into question. Without the large membership base to spread the costs over, these buildings became more of a burden to the Lodges that remained. Of the four buildings shown in this chapter, only the Trenton Masonic Temple remains in the hands of the Freemasons.

The former Paterson Masonic Temple along Broadway was likely one of the largest in the state. Fred Wesley Wentworth, the noted architect responsible for designing much of downtown Paterson, was contracted to design the building in 1923. Wentworth had made a considerable name for himself, and he was elected a Fellow of the American Institute of Architects three years later. The building, done in a Renaissance Revival style, is dominated by a windowless colonnade that spans two stories. Ten blue lodges met in the building by the 1960s, and the complex was active with at least one meeting every night of the week. By 2010, no Lodges were meeting in Paterson, all having merged and moved out of the city. (Above, courtesy of the Newark Public Library; below, courtesy of the Collection of Erich Morgan Huhn.)

The lobby, shown above in a photograph featured in an architectural magazine, was clad in dark marble. The auditorium, below, was done in rich wood trim and included a stage and mezzanine. For the Freemasons meeting in the building, these extra spaces would have been auxiliary to the lodge rooms, which would have been decorated in various styles. The auditoriums and communal spaces like these provided opportunities for the temple association to hold events that could accommodate more than just the individual Lodges, and community events would have been commonplace. The Scottish Rite appendant body Valley of Paterson also used the space. (Both, courtesy of the Newark Public Library.)

The Elizabeth Masonic Temple, on North Broad Street, was built in the 1920s to house the growing Masonic community in the city. The complex was one of several Masonic projects by noted architect Richard G. Schmid. During the building's brief history, it was home to at least seven blue lodges and served as the principal venue for the Elizabeth Philharmonic Orchestra. (Courtesy of the Collection of Erich Morgan Huhn.)

One of the most recognizable Masonic Temples in New Jersey is the Trenton Masonic Temple. After the forgotten Second Masonic Temple of Trenton (pages 30–31) was demolished when the Trenton Banking Company subverted control of the temple association, the Freemasons in Trenton sought to build a modern and stately complex that would rival those of other New Jersey cities. (Courtesy of the Grand Lodge of New Jersey, 1928.)

Army and Navy Masonic Service Center—Masonic Temple, Trenton, New Jersey

The New Trenton Masonic Temple, built on Willow Street (now Barracks Street), was the result of several years of fundraising. Although the temple association was first formed in 1916, World War I interrupted fundraising efforts and were only reassumed in 1921. The organization ultimately raised $800,000 for the construction and furnishing of the building, and the ground breaking occurred in 1926. (Courtesy of the Collection of Erich Morgan Huhn.)

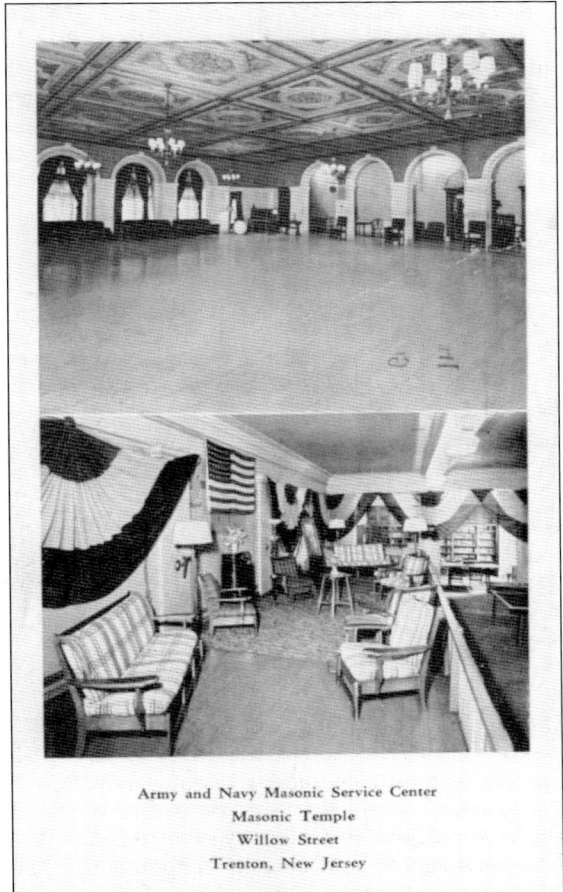

Army and Navy Masonic Service Center
Masonic Temple
Willow Street
Trenton, New Jersey

The building included three lodge rooms, parlors, library, game room, offices, and a large dining room and kitchen. By 1960, seven blue lodges were meeting in the new Masonic temple. During World War II, like many Masonic temples throughout the country, the building served as an Army and Navy Masonic service center for brothers in the armed services. (Courtesy of the Collection of Erich Morgan Huhn.)

Designed in the Neoclassical style by Harry A. Hill and decorated by Gustav Brand, the building features four-foot diameter columns, travertine floors, painted murals, and Masonic detailing throughout. Although Mercer Lodge No. 50 is the only remaining Lodge that actively meets in the building, in 2004, the Grand Lodge purchased the building and began a multiyear restoration and by 2010 had moved offices from Burlington into the building. Together with the Old Masonic

Temple (pages 14–17), which had been moved to the present site at Barrack and West Lafayette Streets, they formed contributing resources to the State House Historic District in the National Register of Historic Places. Although much work remains to be completed, the two properties are excellent examples of the fraternity stepping up and making the preservation of their history a priority. (Courtesy of the Collection of Erich Morgan Huhn.)

The Masonic Temple of Atlantic City at the corner of Ventnor and North Hartford Avenues was one of the last the grand design form of Masonic lodge buildings in New Jersey. Designed by Charles D. Adams, the cornerstone was laid in 1927 after a procession of 1,500 Freemasons down Atlantic Avenue. The building included an auditorium for 1,200 people, dining room, kitchen, caretaker apartment, lounges, offices, game room, library, and two lodge rooms that could each accommodate 180 people. Decorated with marble, terrazzo, and plaster trompe l'oeil, the building cost around $500,000 and was the home to three Lodges at the time of construction. Along with the three original Lodges, one other was formed in the building, and several appendant bodies met in the space. (Courtesy of the Grand Lodge of New Jersey, 1928.)

Seven

POSTWAR BOOM

With the conclusion of World War II, Freemasonry entered a golden age of its own. Fraternalism had seen a huge peak in membership and the establishment of countless different groups between the Civil War and the Great Depression, but it was during this second golden age when Freemasonry specifically saw rapid expansion in popularity. The conservative nature of Freemasonry, the conformist themes of the period, and an attempt to replicate the brotherhood experienced by servicemen have all been cited as causes. In 1949, the grand secretary had reported 89,477 members belonging to 282 Lodges; in 1960, there was a total of 107,680 members with the addition of 8 new Lodges.

Over this period, as after the turn of the century, Masonic Lodges sought to solidify their place in the community by building physical monuments that would endure as symbols of the fraternity's power. As seen throughout American society after World War II, technological developments in building and construction design meant that structures could be built faster and easier than ever before. Aesthetically, changes in taste and design saw the development of Modernist architecture dominated by functionalism and simplified design. At the same time, the proliferation of professionalism as troops returned home and sought respectable white-collar jobs meant that architecture and construction firms popped up throughout the country. While Masonic Temples that were once ornately decorated and designed by noted architects, the new form of postwar Masonic temples would be utilitarian community centers in a conformist world.

The form would be dominated by simple and unadorned buildings typically of brick or concrete construction. Inexpensive to construct with advances in concrete and steel building techniques, Lodges that had previously rented or shared spaces with other Lodges or fraternal organizations took the opportunities to build their own spaces. Between 1950 and 1976, more than 30 Lodges built new homes for themselves. The buildings presented in this chapter show the range in style found within this form of Masonic temple, and while some have been lost, many of the buildings remain home to Lodges today.

The Masonic Temple, built by Silentia Lodge No. 168 in Butler, presents an early adaptation of modern architectural designs. The simple and unadorned façade on Main Street is only broken by a large rectangular door and surround with modern lighting. Along the side façade, the building's modern design continues with small windows and a plain unadorned façade along the second floor where the Lodge Room is located. Silentia Lodge No. 168 is still active at the building, which is also used by the American Legion. (Courtesy of the Grand Lodge of New Jersey, 1956.)

Built in 1956, the Masonic Temple at Cleveland and Highland Avenues in Palmyra became home to Covenant Lodge No. 161. The building's simple brick façade is ornamented with a decorative arched window. At some point, a gabled roof was added over the flat roof, a common maintenance move that often detracts from the design appeal of the building. (Courtesy of the Grand Lodge of New Jersey, 1957.)

The Masonic temple of Teaneck (above) and Pennsauken (below) present two lost lodges of New Jersey. Built on Kenwood Place in the 1950s for Teaneck Lodge No. 274, the building has survived, but the Lodge that met there has since moved and merged. In Pennsauken, the Masonic temple at Merchantville and Jefferson Avenue may have been demolished, but Universal Lodge No. 216 has since moved and merged and eventually helped form USS New Jersey Lodge No. 62 in 2005. The brick and column design of the Pennsauken building present a common attempt to draw in colonial design on an otherwise simple and modern brick structure. (Above, courtesy of the Grand Lodge of New Jersey, 1957; below, courtesy of the Grand Lodge of New Jersey, 1958.)

The Masonic Temple of Swedesboro, at the intersection of Glen Echo Avenue and Franklin Street, was built for Swedesboro Lodge No. 157. The building remains and has been renovated almost indistinguishable, but the Lodge has since moved out. After merging with Paulsboro Lodge (page 84) in 1997, the building was sold. (Courtesy of the Grand Lodge of New Jersey, 1958.)

Pompton Lakes Masonic Temple was built in 1957 for Pompton Lodge No. 246. The building, on Hamburg Turnpike, has been altered considerably and the facade only looks marginally like the original. Pompton Lodge No. 246, warranted in 1923, has since merged with several other Lodges resulting in Genesis Lodge No. 88, which currently meets in the building. (Courtesy of the Grand Lodge of New Jersey, 1958.)

Harmony Lodge No. 18 in Toms River built the Masonic Temple on State Route 37. The building presents a more traditionally designed lodge with colonial-inspired windows and door surrounded with columns and entablature. The Lodge was formed in 1850 and rented several locations before the construction of this building. (Courtesy of the Grand Lodge of New Jersey, 1958.)

The Pitman Masonic Temple was built by Pitman Lodge No. 197 on Lambs Road in 1957. The simple brick exterior, unadorned by ornamentation or fenestration, presents archetypical postwar design principles. Pitman Lodge No. 197 continues to meet in the building and has maintained the mid-century structure in relatively original condition. (Courtesy of the Grand Lodge of New Jersey, 1958.)

The Masonic Temples of Hopewell (above) and Carteret (below) present an interesting example of design choices. Built for Hopewell Lodge No. 155, which has since moved out and merged with Amwell Lodge No. 12 (page 26), the Lodge attempted to cover the modern brick construction with colonial styling. Theodore Roosevelt Lodge No. 219 at Elm Street in Carteret, however, took a more utilitarian approach to their building design, leaving an unadorned front massing with simple fenestration. Built at a cost of $48,000, the building was inaugurated in 1958 and only later were columns and a faux pediment added to the building. (Both, courtesy of the Grand Lodge of New Jersey, 1959.)

Philo Lodge No. 243 built the Masonic Temple of South River in 1958 on Old Bridge Turnpike. Warranted in 1923, the Lodge had rented space and met for a period in a former synagogue before constructing this Mid-Century Modern building. Like many Masonic Lodges, a Level Club was organized as a fundraising organization that helped make the construction of the temple a reality. (Courtesy of the Grand Lodge of New Jersey, 1959.)

The Masonic Temple in Paulsboro was built on Clarksboro Road in 1958 for Paulsboro Lodge No. 262. The simple brick façade remains although once again a gabled roof was added and detracts from the original design. Swedesboro Lodge No. 157 (page 80) merged with the Lodge in 1997 and today is known as Clarksboro Lodge No. 87. (Courtesy of the Grand Lodge of New Jersey, 1959.)

Hereford Lodge No. 177 built the Masonic Temple of Wildwood on Atlantic Avenue in 1960. The building was the realization of 10 years of fundraising efforts, and the cornerstone was brought over from a quarry in Hereford, England. The exterior was done in a rough veneer-style masonry that was popular in the 1960s and 1970s. Later, the Lodge expanded and doubled the size of their building, mirroring the right façade (shown here) off the left of the entrance. The interior photograph below, from a contemporary postcard, shows the design aesthetics of a 1960s Masonic lodge room. Simple, clean lines and the predominance of blue (a design choice that still blights Masonic lodges today) became the setting and replaced the once elaborate lodge rooms of yesteryear. (Above, courtesy of the Grand Lodge of New Jersey, 1961; below, courtesy of the Collection of Erich Morgan Huhn.)

Two surviving examples of the postwar form are evident in Burlington and Bergenfield. The Burlington Masonic Temple opened in 1961 and was built for Burlington Lodge No. 32 on Mount Holly Road. The building was the final home for the Lodge and was built in two stages, with a collation room added in 1972. From the air, the Burlington Temple forms the shape of a Masonic square. The Bergenfield Temple at Windsor Road and Maiden Lane was built in 1961 for William L. Daniels Lodge No. 269. Both buildings' use of glass, brick, and stucco invoke popular ideas of 1960s and 1970s architecture. Although Burlington Lodge members still meet in their building, William L. Daniels Lodge has since moved out, and the building's characteristic fenestration has been removed. (Above, courtesy of the Grand Lodge of New Jersey, 1961; below, courtesy of the Grand Lodge of New Jersey, 1962.)

Both built in 1961, the Masonic Temples of Union (above) and Highland Park (below) show more of the typical simple approach to the postwar form. Gavel Lodge No. 273 built the Union Masonic Temple on Morris Avenue, and the building continues to be used by the descendant Lodges that had resulted from several merges over the next four decades; Loyalty Lodge No. 33 is the most recent incantation of the Lodges. The Highland Park Masonic Temple, formerly on North Third Street, was built for Highland Park Lodge No. 240. The Highland Park Masonic Temple, with inset dark brick façade and decorative cast block vertical bans, was demolished, and the Lodge merged with Union Lodge No. 19 in New Brunswick. (Both, courtesy of the Grand Lodge of New Jersey, 1962.)

The Masonic Temple of Pennington, on Burd Street, was built in the 1960s for Cyrus Lodge No. 148. The building employs a more traditional design than other contemporary examples, with a three-bay design delineated in brick and stucco. In 1999, Trenton Lodge No. 5 merged with Cyrus Lodge and formed Trenton-Cyrus Lodge No. 5, which still meets in the building. (Courtesy of the Grand Lodge of New Jersey, 1962.)

Overlook Temple on South Gate Road in New Providence was built as the home of Overlook Lodge No. 163. The building's windowless façade is only delineated by plain brick pilasters that run the entire perimeter. In 1986, Overlook Lodge and Congdon Lodge No. 201 were consolidated to form Congdon-Overlook Lodge No. 163 that now meets in Bernardsville. (Courtesy of the Grand Lodge of New Jersey, 1963.)

The Masonic Temple of Elmer was built in 1962 for the brothers of Elmer Lodge No. 160. The simply designed building at the corner of Chestnut Street and Garrison Road looks more like a home than a Masonic Lodge building. The building remains, and the brothers of Elmer Lodge continue to meet in the space. (Courtesy of the Grand Lodge of New Jersey, 1963.)

The Masonic temple in Cape May Court House was built on Main Street in 1963 by the members of Arbutus Lodge No. 170. The building remains and has since been converted from Masonic to commercial use after Arbutus Lodge merged with Cannon Lodge No. 104 in South Seaville. (Courtesy of the Grand Lodge of New Jersey, 1964.)

Belmar's Masonic temple was built in 1964 for Ocean Lodge No. 89 presents an excellent example of lost Mid-Century Modern design. Located at Maxwell Drive, the building's simple stucco design with modernist fenestration and projecting entrance awning presented a simple but imposing design. Ocean Lodge has moved to Spring Lake Heights and is still active. (Courtesy of the Grand Lodge of New Jersey, 1964.)

The Mantua Masonic Temple was built as the home to Mantua Lodge No. 95. The building's functionalist design is highlighted in this photo that shows the exposed cinderblock construction, a key feature of that design concept. The building is still occupied by Mantua Lodge, which remains active. (Courtesy of the Grand Lodge of New Jersey, 1965.)

The Masonic temple of High Bridge, located on Ridge Road, was built for the members of Hobart Lodge No. 175. Warranted in 1901, Hobart Lodge previously met in the Rialto Theatre on Main Street. In 1960, Hobart Lodge and Hobart Chapter No. 63, Order of the Eastern Star, established a temple association and began fundraising efforts toward the goal of building a Masonic temple. Through public dinners and 50/50s, the temple association quickly raised the funds and purchased four lots at the corner of Dennis Avenue and Ridge Road. The first phase of construction was completed with the first floor in 1962 and allowed the fundraising efforts to continue in the makeshift collation room. By 1963, the building was completed, and Hobart Lodge and Hobart Chapter both moved into the new structure. Hobart Lodge was soon joined by Stewart Lodge No. 34 and Lebonon Lodge No. 6, all three of whom have since consolidated to form Host Lodge No. 6, which continues to meet in the building. (Courtesy of the Grand Lodge of New Jersey, 1965.)

Andover's Masonic temple was built in 1964 by the members of Harmony Lodge No. 8. One of the oldest Lodges in the state, Harmony Lodge was formed in 1788 and went dark for a period during the Morgan Affair. Harmony Lodge moved into the building, on Route 206, after renting out spaces for nearly 200 years. Harmony Lodge still meets in the building. (Courtesy of the Grand Lodge of New Jersey, 1965.)

The Pennsauken Masonic Temple on Park Avenue was built in 1965 for the members of Merchantville Lodge No. 119. Although designed in a Modern style, the members have since added more colonial features, like a columned entry and gabled roof. Merchantville Lodge still meets in the building. (Courtesy of the Grand Lodge of New Jersey, 1966.)

The Masonic temple of Cape May, on Seashore Road, is another example of inauspicious design in the postwar form. It was built in 1965 for the members of Cape Island Lodge No. 30. Before building the Masonic Temple on Seashore Road, the Lodge had met at several locations, including the Odd Fellows Hall. When their previous building was damaged in the Ash Wednesday Storm of 1962, the members met in the space rented by Arbutus Lodge No. 170 in Cape May Court House and began planning to construct a building of their own. After breaking ground in 1965 and moving in a year later, the members took only seven years to retire the mortgage and, in the 1980s, added more rooms off the back of the building. (Courtesy of the Grand Lodge of New Jersey, 1967.)

The Riverside Masonic Temple, on South Chester Avenue in Riverside, was built for the members of Riverside Lodge No. 187. The variegated brick façade of the building's front massing has been preserved with the addition of a gabled roof over the entrance. Beverly Lodge No. 107 consolidated with Riverside in 2000 to form Beverly-Riverside Lodge No. 107. (Courtesy of the Grand Lodge of New Jersey, 1967.)

Kittatinny Lodge No. 164 built the Masonic Temple of Branchville in 1968. Warranted in 1890, the Lodge remains active in the area. The Masonic Temple, on Route 206, is done in a simple and unadorned style like other buildings shown in this chapter. (Courtesy of the Grand Lodge of New Jersey, 1969.)

Throughout this period of expansion, cornerstone laying and dedications played an important ceremonial and social role in Masonic life. In this photograph from 1974, Grand Master Vernon Cornine spreads mortar at the laying of the cornerstone for Kane Lodge No. 55's new building in Hanover. As explained earlier, the ceremony is one of the few rituals that can be done in public and often involves a large retinue from Grand Lodge officers. Beyond consecrating the stone with corn, wine, and oil, the Elected Line of the Grand Lodge test the cornerstone by the square, level, and plumb, all of which are important symbols of their respective offices and Freemasonry. Kane Lodge, previously in Newark (page 46), moved to Hanover, like many Lodges that followed members out to the suburbs as New Jersey developed in the postwar period. This meant an expansion of Lodges in suburban communities would lead to a general decline of Freemasonry in major cities, a problem that has only recently been addressed. (Courtesy of the Grand Lodge of New Jersey, 1974.)

The Masonic Temple on Old Budd Lake Road in Budd Lake was built in 1973 for the members of Musconetcong Lodge No. 151. Shown here still under construction, the temple was done in a Modern-design treatment with low angled roof and variegated brick masonry, with clear, sleek design lines typical of the period. The building is still used by the Lodge. (Courtesy of the Grand Lodge of New Jersey, 1974.)

Samaritan Lodge No. 98 built this Masonic temple in the 1970s on Route 94 in Hardyston. The Lodge had been founded in 1869 but surrendered its warrant in 2013. The building remains but has been largely renovated and converted into a commercial property. (Courtesy of the Grand Lodge of New Jersey, 1976.)

The Westfield Masonic Temple, shown here draped in bunting at the cornerstone dedication in 1976, was built by the members of Atlas Lodge No. 125. After their former building on Temple Place (page 67) had been destroyed in a fire, the members met in Scotch Plains for several years while planning the construction of a new building. After fundraising and planning, the new Masonic Temple was built along Central Avenue. The building was done with a blend of features to create a generic 1970s design with some colonial detailing (obscured by in this photograph by the pavilion). The building was one of the last of the postwar building boom in New Jersey. New Atlas Lodge remains in the building, although several Lodges have since been merged or consolidated to create Atlas-Pythagoras Lodge No. 10. The Westfield Masonic Temple is home to eight appendant bodies ranging from the Knights Templar and Royal Arch Masons to the National Sojourners and DeMolay. (Courtesy of the Grand Lodge of New Jersey, 1976.)

Eight

BEYOND THE BLUE LODGE

Although the blue lodges that have been shown in the preceding chapters are the local incarnations of Freemasonry throughout the country, there are countless other organizations and levels that add to the diversity of Masonic culture. The Grand Lodge, which serves as the corporate body that organizes and authorizes local Lodges is just one of many groups beyond the Blue Lodge. Of these groups, several appendant bodies come to mind as some of the most popular branches of Freemasonry. While the list of groups is ever growing as new orders and degrees are established and introduced, there have been a handful of organizations that have added to the built environment of New Jersey Freemasonry.

Directly related to the blue lodges of New Jersey is the Grand Lodge, and the efforts started in the late 1890s to establish for members a home for the aged. Even though fraternal charity had always been a key tenet of the organization, the trend of "Masonic homes" emerged throughout the country in the late 19th century. Compounded by efforts to establish an orphanage, the Grand Lodge of New Jersey formed the Masonic Home in Burlington in 1898. Although the orphanage has since ceased operations, the Masonic Home remains as a nursing and retirement community supported by New Jersey Freemasons.

Outside the auspices of the Grand Lodge, appendant bodies are considered independent organizations that are closely affiliated with Freemasonry and expand on Masonic teachings and rituals. While the list may seem endless, the more prominent of these groups are the Order of the Eastern Star, Scottish Rite, and the Shrine. Formed in the Antebellum South, the Eastern Star has transformed into an international organization for female members of the Masonic community. The Scottish Rite and Shrine were both formed in the 19th century and have helped raise funds for countless charitable causes, most notably the Shriners Hospitals for Children.

With the rise and fall of fraternalism and Freemasonry throughout the last 250 years, the built environment that has survived provides an important insight into the impact these groups have had on the lives of both members and the community at large.

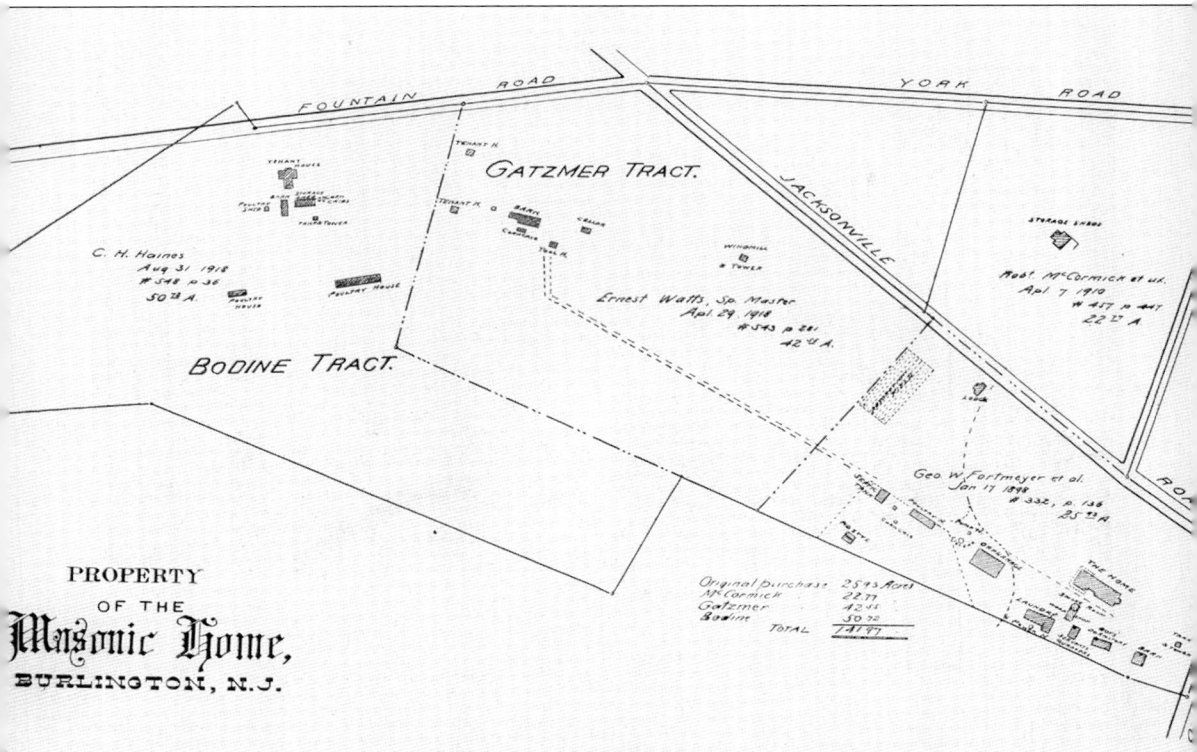

The map contains the following labels:

FOUNTAIN ROAD

YORK ROAD

GATZMER TRACT.

JACKSONVILLE

TENANT H.

C. H. Haines
Aug 31 1918
548 p 36
50 ¾ A.

POULTRY HOUSE

STORAGE SHEDS

Rob.ᵗ McCormick et ux.
Apl 7 1910
457 p 467
22 ¾ A.

WINDMILL
& TOWER

Ernest Watts, Sp. Master
Apl 29 1918
543 p 201
42 ⁴ A.

BODINE TRACT.

Geo W. Fortmayer et al.
Jan 17 1898
332, p 136
25 ¾ A.

PROPERTY
OF THE
Masonic Home,
BURLINGTON, N.J.

Original purchase   25 45 Acres
McCormick   22.77
Gatzmer   42 ⁴⁴
Bodine   50 ⁷²
        TOTAL   141 47

The Masonic Home of New Jersey was a project long in the making. As New Jersey developed through the end of the 19th century, new answers for charitable care were needed as an increasing population sought social and charitable relief. For Freemasonry, charity had largely been disbursed by local Lodges, but long-term solutions were needed to help support members in their advanced age. To this end, the Grand Lodge of New Jersey, like so many Grand Lodges throughout the country, established the Masonic home in 1898. A committee had purchased the property in Burlington, shown on this map labeled "Geo W Fortmayer," of 26 acres and a stone home for $24,927. In 1910, a farm property across the street was also purchased, and two additional farms were purchased by 1918, bringing to total acreage of the site just short of 142 acres. The site has grown over the last 100 years and, today, totals 450 acres, including the original track. (Courtesy of the Grand Lodge of New Jersey, 1929.)

Masonic Home, Burlington, N. J.

The home that was one the site when it was purchased by the Grand Lodge was an impressive stone mansion with mansard roof. The Italianate styling of the building was likely built between 1850 and 1870s, when that design treatment was in vogue. Typical for healthcare facilities of the period, the building was nestled among gardens and woodlands with large windows that would provide fresh air and sunlight. (Courtesy of the Collection of Erich Morgan Huhn.)

This collage, from the 1898 Grand Lodge *Proceedings*, shows the officers and members of the Grand Lodge in January for a reception at the newly acquired Masonic home. In a time when individuals were expected to work until death and without social security nets, the Masonic home provided an opportunity for aged individuals with limited means to live out their days in dignity. (Courtesy of the Grand Lodge of New Jersey, 1898.)

The old home was one of four principal living structures on the property, including the orphanage (page 108), boys' dormitory, and servant quarters. Converting private homes like this into homes for the aged was a popular solution to the growing demand for charitable aid, and in New Jersey, the Freemasons were not alone in establishing a home, and institutions like this popped up across the state and country. (Courtesy of the Grand Lodge of New Jersey, 1898.)

At the time of opening, the original building became home to 23 "guests," and while the original intention was to provide aid to the aged, one orphan was listed in residence in the first annual report to the Grand Lodge. After two years, it was decided to build an addition that would house 80 more. (Courtesy of the Grand Lodge of New Jersey, 1898.)

Although the home was meant as a charitable institution, the bucolic setting was as much a healthy choice as a financial one. New Jersey, known as the Garden State because of the importance of truck agriculture, had an impressive agricultural industry through the turn of the century. Setting the Masonic home in Burlington amidst rolling farmland enabled the managers to offset the upkeep costs through the sale of produce and renting out farmland. This proved to be a convenient and profitable exchange and continued through the first half of the 20th century. Outbuildings on the site included a greenhouse, entrance lodge, laundry, workhouse, and barn (shown on the right below). Of all the original buildings, the barn is the only one that remains. (Both, courtesy of the Grand Lodge of New Jersey, 1898.)

The orphanage was established on the campus of the Masonic home early on and was eventually run out of this building. Just as the thought was to surround the infirmed with fresh air and sunlight, the prevailing theories on orphanage management meant the late 19th and early 20th century saw an increase in the establishment of orphanages in the countryside. Children who were either orphaned or whose parents could not afford to raise them would send children to orphanages like these, where the children could enjoy the outdoors and be away from the corrupting influences of city life. Orphanages like these were popular forms of charity by fraternal organizations and sprung up throughout the country. The home, now demolished, was done in a handsome brick Colonial Revival style that was popular during the period. By 1910, the orphanage was home to about 25 children. (Courtesy of the Collection of Erich Morgan Huhn.)

As with most orphanages at the time, the Masonic Orphans' Home offered a wide range of curricular and extracurricular activities. For academics, children were sent to the local schools in Burlington. The Masonic Home Band (above), a coed children's band, was created to encourage music education among the children. The band would travel around the state giving concerts to raise funds. At the same time, domestic education was instilled through home economics courses. To help promote funding for the orphanage, the public and members of the fraternity were welcome to see displays of sewing, basketry, and other goods that the children were taught to produce. (Courtesy of the Grand Lodge of New Jersey, 1924.)

In 1926, construction was started on a new dormitory for boys. The new building was part of a large expansion of the Masonic Home campus and was located at the corner of Jacksonville and Oxmeade Roads. Completed the next year, the building's plain brick design is typical of institutional architecture from the period. Although the orphanage was established and funded by the Freemasons, the children in attendance were not required to have any family connections to the fraternity. As the orphanage system of child services became unpopular toward the middle of the 20th century, the Freemasons disbanded the New Jersey Masonic Orphans' Home and repurposed the buildings to support the expanding Masonic Home. The Boys' Home is the only remaining structure associated with the orphanage operation on the campus and has been extensively renovated to serve as the home to Acacia Hospice. (Courtesy of the Grand Lodge of New Jersey, 1926.)

BOYS' HOMES, MASONIC HOME, BURLINGTON, N. J.

Although orphanages have fallen out of favor, institutions like the Boys' Home played an important role in establishing a social-welfare net. Benefit societies like the Eagles and the Odd Fellows had express promises of financial benefits to membership. Charity has played an important role in Freemasonry from the earliest days, but inherent benefits have been almost unanimously rejected by all Grand Lodges. The Masonic home and the Masonic Orphans' Home were part of a broader change at the end of the 19th century to provide modern charitable relief to members and the community. (Above, courtesy of the Collection of Erich Morgan Huhn; below, courtesy of the Grand Lodge of New Jersey, 1927.)

MASONIC HOME, BURLINGTON, N. J.

By the 1920s, the Masonic Home had reached capacity, and the Grand Lodge was forced to investigate building larger quarters for the operation. In 1925, the plans came to fruition with the completion of the new Masonic home. The new building was centered over the foundation of the original Masonic home and nearly tripled the space available for aging members. The building was done in a similar institutional design style as the Boys' Home (pages 112–113). The campus has been significantly expanded over the last 90 years but the façade of the main building, dubbed the David Brearley Memorial Building, has been largely preserved. The 1920s main building forms the nucleus of the Masonic home campus, even to this day, and serves as a symbol of Masonic charity throughout the state. (Courtesy of the Collection of Erich Morgan Huhn.)

The Shirrefs Memorial was added in 1927 by the Scottish Rite to commemorate the late Robert A. Shirrefs. Shirrefs had served as grand secretary general and deputy for New Jersey to the Scottish Rite and was made a 33rd-degree member of the Scottish Rite. The memorial remains and is the main entrance to the Masonic home. (Courtesy of the Collection of Erich Morgan Huhn.)

The North Entrance, visible on the far right of the postcard on the preceding page, shows a closer view of the architectural detailing of the building. The simple white colonial-styled columns and railing along the entrance portico and the simple brick pilasters break the perimeter of the building's first two floors. The cast-stone cornice between the second and third floors and regular fenestration pattern add to the building's imposing form and massing. (Courtesy of the Grand Lodge of New Jersey, 1925.)

Through the Great Depression, the Masonic Home, like all charitable organizations, faced increased demand. Additions were made to the main building, including this solarium on top of the South Porch and renovations throughout the building. This simple addition was dedicated in 1939. (Courtesy of the Grand Lodge of New Jersey, 1940.)

CENTER DRIVE AND MAIN ENTRANCE, MASONIC HOME, BURLINGTON, N. J.

The new Masonic Home provided a more spacious campus for the guests. Still nestled in the rolling countryside, the new building provided more amenities than the old, outdated home. Along the main entrance hall, there were parlors and a library where guests could entertain visitors and socialize. To support the Masonic Home, the Freemasons throughout the state helped fund the construction through annual contributions. At the same time, the farmland surrounding the Masonic Home continued to provide income and fresh produce for the guests. (Both, courtesy of the Collection of Erich Morgan Huhn.)

MAIN ENTRANCE HALL, MASONIC HOME, BURLINGTON, N. J.

FIRST FLOOR LOBBY, MASONIC HOME, BURLINGTON, N. J.

The parlors and lobby on the first floor of the Masonic Home were just some of the amenities. An auditorium was built that allowed for the Masonic home to hold public events, movies, and Masonic meetings. A dining room and other spaces meant that living in the home would be akin to staying at a resort, and the staff helped ensure that the guests were able to enjoy even extended stays. Postcards like these were popular souvenirs for guests to send to friends and family and provided a small revenue for the upkeep of the home. (Both, courtesy of the Collection of Erich Morgan Huhn.)

AUDITORIUM, MASONIC HOME, BURLINGTON, N. J.

The Charles A. Eisenfelder Medical Complex was added to the Masonic Home in the 1970s. Named after a member from Nutley Lodge No. 25, who served as Grand Master in 1969, the addition provided more space for nursing staff and patients. The additions have since been incorporated into further development at the Masonic home. As demands changed, the nursing sections of the Masonic Home have been slowly renovated and upgraded into a retirement community. The current Masonic Home, with the Brearley Memorial preserved and a sprawling campus surrounding it, contains several stages of care for residents. Along with the Masonic Home, the Grand Lodge briefly managed another retirement community called Acacia-Lumberton Manor in Lumberton, New Jersey. Though the Acacia-Lumberton Manor has since been sold off, the Grand Lodge continues to invest in the Masonic Home and has recently broken ground on an expanded retirement cottage community. (Courtesy of the Collection of Erich Morgan Huhn.)

Eastern Star Home, Bernardsville, N.J.

Although the Order of the Eastern Star did not build any of their own meeting spaces, the organization early on established a home for elderly members. Much like the Masonic home shown in the previous chapter, the Eastern Star home was opened to use of any member that required it and was funded through the generosity of the membership. The Bernardsville home shown here has since been sold, and the Eastern Star dedicated a new home in Bridgewater in 1959. The new home is still run by the Eastern Star and serves just under 100 elderly members. (Courtesy of the Collection of Erich Morgan Huhn.)

Main Entrance, Eastern Star Home, Bernardsville, N.J.

Better known as the Krueger, or Krueger-Scott Mansion, the Scottish Rite owned the impressive home for a short time. Built in 1888 by German American brewer Gottfried Krueger for $250,000, the home was reportedly one of the most expensive and lavish residences in the city. The Scottish Rite purchased the property in 1926 for $100,000 and added a 700-seat auditorium while converting the home into a clubhouse for the members. As part of their renovations, the Scottish Rite added symbolic motifs throughout the house. In 1958, as the demographics of Newark shifted and members of the Scottish Rite moved to the suburbs, the fraternity sold the building to Louise Scott. Scott had made a name for herself as the first as the city's first black female millionaires through her successful beauty product businesses. She converted the building into a beauty school, private residence, and later, an African American community and cultural center. The City of Newark took over the project in the 1990s but quickly abandoned the property. (Courtesy of the Newark Public Library.)

SCOTTISH RITE TEMPLE, VALLEY OF CAMDEN, NEW JERSEY
WHITE HORSE PIKE AND MAGILL AVENUE, WEST COLLINGSWOOD, N. J.

Originally built in the 1860s by a wealthy businessman, the Excelsior Scottish Rite Temple of Collingswood has had a long and varied history. The building had previously been a residence and hospital. The Scottish Rite purchased the building in 1930 for $125,000. The auditorium at the Excelsior Scottish Rite Temple was added as part of a 1931 Art Deco addition. Designed by Henry Allen of Camden, the addition included an auditorium of 1,050 seats and a large ballroom below. Unlike Blue Lodge rituals, Scottish Rite rituals are presented to initiates in the form of a play. (Courtesy of the Collection of Erich Morgan Huhn.)

SCOTTISH RITE TEMPLE, VALLEY OF CAMDEN, NEW JERSEY
WHITE HORSE PIKE AND MAGILL AVENUE, WEST COLLINGSWOOD, N. J.
Our parking lot covers an area of 14,540 square yards. It has been enlarged for your convenience on
the fourth Friday evenings from September to June inclusive, as well as special occasions.

Through an agreement with the Borough of Collingswood, the nonprofit Collingswood Foundation for the Arts manages events and concerts. The auditorium, marketed as the Scottish Rite Auditorium, is an important arts center in South Jersey and represents a successful partnership between the fraternity and the public. (Courtesy of the Collection of Erich Morgan Huhn.)

SCOTTISH RITE TEMPLE   UNITED CONTRACTORS CORPORATION, BUILDERS
JERSEY CITY, N. J.   JERSEY CITY, N. J.

The Scottish Rite Temple, home to the Valley of Jersey City and built in 1908, was one of five "valleys," or administrative districts, in New Jersey. It is the oldest and only purpose-built Scottish Rite building in the state and was designed by prominent local architect John T. Rowland Jr. The Scottish Rite moved out in the 1970s. (Courtesy of the Collection of Erich Morgan Huhn.)

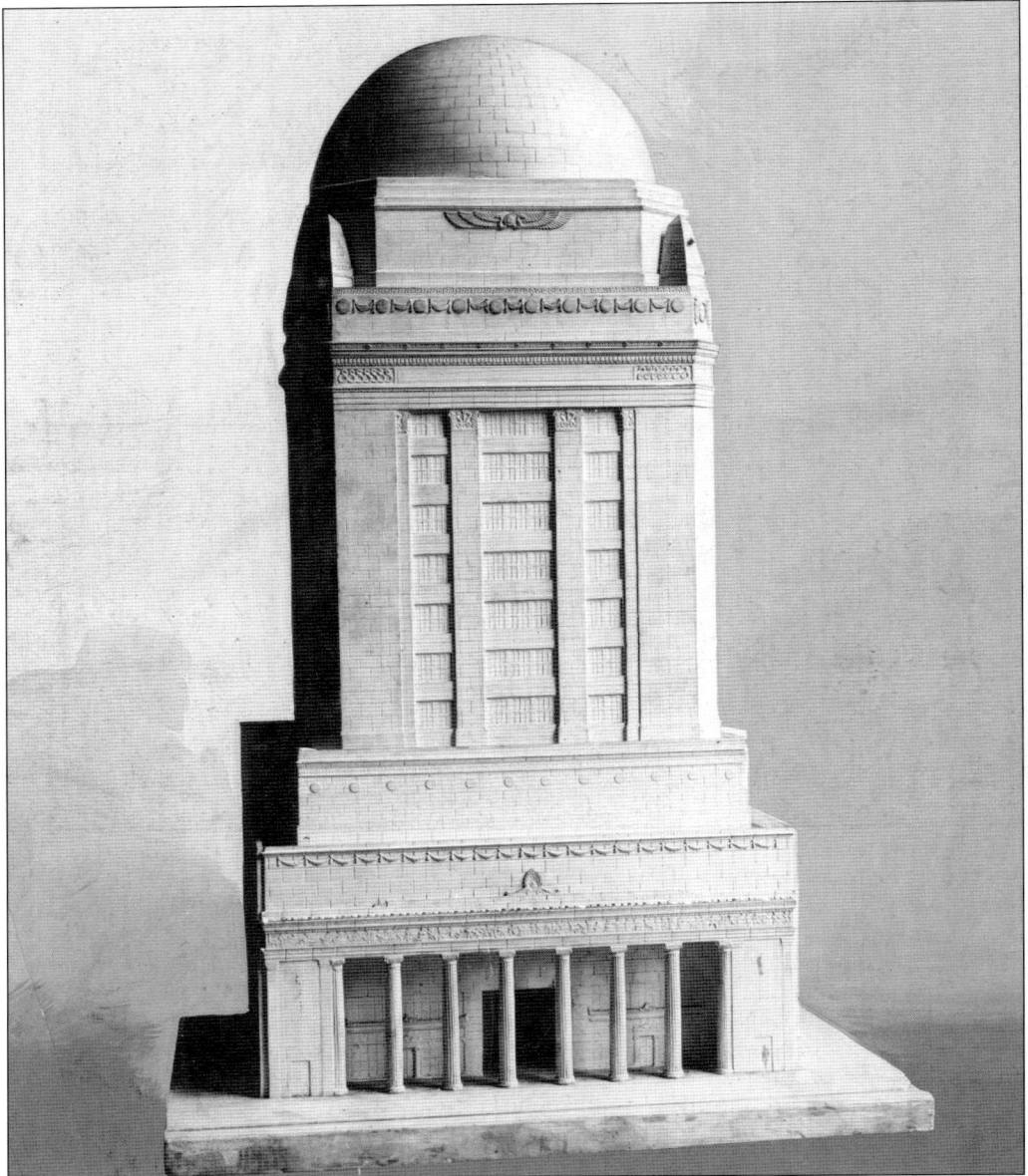

Noted architects Frank Grad, Henry Baechlin, and George Backoff collaborated on the designs for the Salaam Shrine Temple. To finance the construction, the Shriners had formed the Salaam Temple Realty Corporation and broke ground in 1922. In 1925, the lower four-floor theater section had been completed and was dedicated with a large ceremony, where it was announced that a large office tower would be erected over the building. Because of costs, the tower never became a reality. With the Great Depression, the Salaam Shriners faced financial troubles and were forced to sell the hall for $1.4 million at a sheriff's sale in 1933 to the Prudential Life Insurance Company. The building then ran through a series of owners until the City of Newark purchased the property in 1964. Salaam Shrine had since moved out of Newark, and the group had been meeting in Livingston. (Courtesy of the Newark Public Library.)

Early on, the Salaam Shrine Temple became known as the Mosque Theatre. The building's 3,500-seat auditorium was one of the largest in the state and surpassed Carnegie Hall and the Metropolitan Opera House at Lincoln Center. Atop the capacity and the 70-foot stage, the auditorium has excellent acoustics that have been praised by artists and conductors. Below the theater, the building also contains a 2,000-seat ballroom and catering hall. Countless artists and shows have been put on in the space, which was one of the leading venues in the state through to the completion of the New Jersey Performing Arts Center just down the street. The building was also the home of New Jersey's first television station, which broadcast from the auditorium and had a studio on the site. When the city took over the building, it was renamed Newark Symphony Hall. (Courtesy of the Newark Public Library.)

This photograph shows the officers and members of the Grand Lodge standing in front of the old Crescent Mosque on North Clinton Avenue at the cornerstone laying for the new Mosque in 1928. After the Shriners had moved into the New Crescent Mosque across the street, the Scottish Rite Valley of Trenton took up residence. (Courtesy of the Grand Lodge of New Jersey, 1929.)

T-20—(A. A. O. N. M. S. Mosque) Crescent Shrine Temple, Trenton, N. J.

The New Crescent Mosque, on North Clinton Avenue in Trenton, was finished in 1929 and done in an ornate Moorish Revival style by architect Walter Hankin. The building included an auditorium that sat 4,000 and a banquet hall with room for 2,600 and was reportedly one of the largest Shriners buildings at the time of completion. (Courtesy of the Collection of Erich Morgan Huhn.)

BIBLIOGRAPHY

Berman, Ric. *Foundations: Celebrating the Tercentenary of the Premier Grand Lodge, 1717–2017*, Great Heath, Oxon.: The Old Stables Press, 2015.

Bullock, Steven C. *Revolutionary Brotherhood: Freemasonry and the Transformation of the American Social Order, 1730–1840*, Chapel Hill: Omohundro Institute of Early American History and Culture, 1996.

Carnes, Mark C. *Secret Ritual and Manhood in Victorian America*, New Haven: Yale University Press, 1989.

Huss, Wayne A. *The Master Builders: A History of the Grand Lodge of Free and Accepted Masons of Pennsylvania* [3 vol.], Philadelphia: Grand Lodge of Pennsylvania, 1986.

Jacob, Margaret C. *The Origins of Freemasonry: Facts & Fictions*, Philadelphia: University of Pennsylvania Press, 2007.

Lipson, Dorothy Ann. *Freemasonry in Federalist Connecticut, 1789–1835*, Princeton: Princeton University Press, 1977.

Moore, William D. and Tabbert, Mark A. *Secret Societies in America: Foundational Studies of Fraternalism*, New Orleans: Cornerstone Book Publishers, 2011.

Moore, William D. *Masonic Temples: Freemasonry, Ritual Architecture, and Masculine Archetypes*. Knoxville: University of Tennessee Press, 2006.

New Jersey, Grand Lodge of. *A History of The Grand Lodge of the Most Ancient and Honorable Society of Free and Accepted Masons for the State of New Jersey: Commemorating the 175th Anniversary, 1786–1961*, Trenton: Grand Lodge of New Jersey, 1961.

New Jersey, Grand Lodge of. *History of Freemasonry in New Jersey: Commemorating the Two Hundredth Anniversary Of the Organization of the Grand Lodge of The Most Ancient and Honorable Society of Free and Accepted Masons for the State of New Jersey, 1786–1987*, Trenton: Grand Lodge of New Jersey, 1987.

New Jersey, Grand Lodge. *Proceedings of The Grand Lodge of the Most Ancient and Honorable Society of Free and Accepted Masons for the State of New Jersey*, Trenton: Grand Lodge of New Jersey, various years.

Tatsch, J. Hugo. *Freemasonry in the Thirteen Colonies*, New York: Macoy Publishing and Masonic Supply Company, 1933.

Warburton, Frederick R. *Masonic Home Boy*. New York: Vantage Press, 1971.

INDEX

ABOUT THE

ORGANIZATION

The Grand Lodge of the Most Ancient and Honorable Society of Free and Accepted Masons for the State of New Jersey was formed in 1786. As the Grand Lodge with jurisdiction over New Jersey, the organization is charged with establishing and promoting Freemasonry within the state. Even before the founding of the Grand Lodge, Freemasonry has played an important role in the social and cultural life of New Jersey. Since forming the Grand Lodge, countless brothers have been raised through the ritual degrees of Freemasonry and supported the key tenets of brotherly love, relief, and truth.

The organization continues through to this day, supporting various charitable causes on the local, state, and national levels. Through appendant bodies like the Scottish Rite and the Shriners, Freemasons give millions of dollars each year to charities like Dyslexia Learning Centers and the Shriners Hospitals for Children.

Beyond the charitable support, Freemasonry has continued the long tradition of spreading the light of Enlightenment teachings to men from all walks of life. For Freemasonry, the mantra "to be one, ask one," has always been true; membership is drawn from all walks of life. As the world's oldest fraternity moves into the 21st century, Freemasonry is on stable ground throughout the Garden State in no small part because of the work done by the Grand Lodge of New Jersey.

Discover Thousands of Local History Books
Featuring Millions of Vintage Images

Arcadia Publishing, the leading local history publisher in the United States, is committed to making history accessible and meaningful through publishing books that celebrate and preserve the heritage of America's people and places.

Find more books like this at
www.arcadiapublishing.com

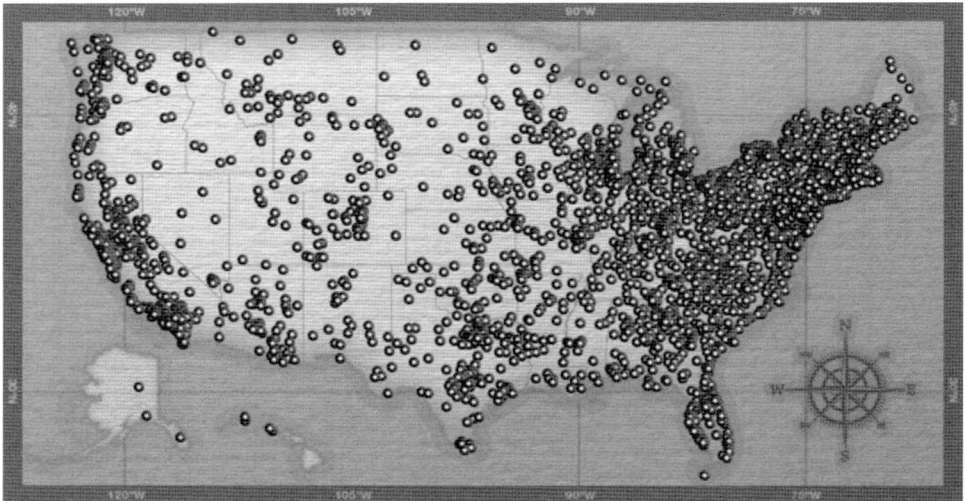

Search for your hometown history, your old stomping grounds, and even your favorite sports team.